# Retail Sales

# For Network Marketers

## How To Get New Customers For Your MLM Business

KEITH & TOM "BIG AL" SCHREITER

*Retail Sales for Network Marketers*
© 2017 by Keith & Tom "Big Al" Schreiter

Published by Fortune Network Publishing
PO Box 890084
Houston, TX 77289 USA
Telephone: +1 (281) 280-9800

ISBN-10: 1-892366-84-3

ISBN-13: 978-1-892366-84-9

# Contents

Get new customers now. . . . . . . . . . . . . . . . . . . . . . . . . . . . . .v

Mindset #1: How our network marketing business really works. . . . .1

Mindset #2: How to instantly get rid of our fear of selling. . . . . . .5

Mindset #3: Many people already want what we sell. . . . . . . . . .7

Mindset #4: Shy? Welcome to the club. . . . . . . . . . . . . . . . . .9

Finding people who want to buy. . . . . . . . . . . . . . . . . . . . .17

Afraid to talk about your products? . . . . . . . . . . . . . . . . . . .19

Code words for "No!" . . . . . . . . . . . . . . . . . . . . . . . . . . . .23

Using a "tiny question" first. . . . . . . . . . . . . . . . . . . . . . . .29

What can we say next? . . . . . . . . . . . . . . . . . . . . . . . . . . .39

Treating humans ... as humans. . . . . . . . . . . . . . . . . . . . . .45

Sound bites. . . . . . . . . . . . . . . . . . . . . . . . . . . . . . . . . .49

Be specific. . . . . . . . . . . . . . . . . . . . . . . . . . . . . . . . . . .61

Use the big "If" word to grab attention. . . . . . . . . . . . . . . . .65

Words that kill. . . . . . . . . . . . . . . . . . . . . . . . . . . . . . . . .71

People don't really want to buy things. . . . . . . . . . . . . . . . . .81

Keeping it simple. . . . . . . . . . . . . . . . . . . . . . . . . . . . . . .87

Here is the short story. . . . . . . . . . . . . . . . . . . . . . . . . . . .91

Ask open-ended questions. . . . . . . . . . . . . . . . . . . . . . . . .95

You have to love Girl Scout cookies. . . . . . . . . . . . . . . . . . . .97

Practice descriptive words ... before we speak. . . . . . . . . . . . 105

The power of social proof. . . . . . . . . . . . . . . . . . . . . . . . . 113

Before we buy advertising. . . . . . . . . . . . . . . . . . . . . . . . . 121

Where do I find more customers to talk to? . . . . . . . . . . . . . 125

Do you have personal experience with the product? . . . . . . . . 137

Create interest with a quiz. . . . . . . . . . . . . . . . . . . . . . . . . 141

Remember this? . . . . . . . . . . . . . . . . . . . . . . . . . . . . . . . 145

Great ideas to add more sales. . . . . . . . . . . . . . . . . . . . . . . 147

And finally. . . . . . . . . . . . . . . . . . . . . . . . . . . . . . . . . . . 155

Thank you. . . . . . . . . . . . . . . . . . . . . . . . . . . . . . . . . . . 157

More Big Al Books . . . . . . . . . . . . . . . . . . . . . . . . . . . . . . 159

About The Authors . . . . . . . . . . . . . . . . . . . . . . . . . . . . . 161

# GET NEW CUSTOMERS NOW.

Retail sales generate instant profits. What a great way to start off our network marketing business.

Satisfied customers create a steady monthly recurring income. All we have to do is allow our customers to buy, and service them as needed. However, you might be thinking:

- But I am not a salesman.
- I don't feel good about selling to my friends.
- What do I say?
- What if the people I talk to say "No" to me?
- I don't know anybody!

No problem. We can learn.

We learned how to use a smartphone. We learned how to order food from a menu. So learning the skills to make retail sales in our network marketing business can be easy as well.

## How can we learn
## to create retail sales?

Easy.

There are two things we will learn that will create continuous retail sales.

1.  Create a new mindset so we will enjoy retailing.

2.  Learn exactly what to say and do to create new customers.

Let's learn how to change our mindset in the next few chapters, and then we'll move on to the great things we will say and do to create retail customers on-demand.

Ready to get started?

**Important note:** In this book, we will use the word "products" even though we will be describing products **and** services. So if you sell services, just substitute the word "services" when appropriate.

# MINDSET #1:
# HOW OUR NETWORK MARKETING BUSINESS REALLY WORKS.

Do you have goals, desires, motivation, needs, vision boards? That's not enough.

We need to deliver value in return for our commissions.

- Our network marketing company does not pay commissions based on our efforts.

- Our network marketing company does not pay commissions based on our needs.

- Our network marketing company pays commissions based on results only.

This is NOT a job where we receive a paycheck for hours worked. This is our own business. We receive commissions based upon our results. Our network marketing company pays us on the value we bring to them through our customers.

### So it is all about results.

Here is the big picture.

A network marketing company can be in the nutrition business, the skincare business, the utilities business, the natural products business, the travel business, etc.

We are not part of the company. We don't work in customer service. We don't mail out invoices and bills. We are not picking secret herbs underneath rocks in China at midnight with leprechauns to put them into a special formulation. We don't even put skincare creams inside the jars or apply the labels.

Our network marketing company does all of this for us. They provide the website, brochures, and they can service customers without us. Plus, we don't want to be part of our network marketing company, because this would be yet another job!

Our company can do everything except ... get people to make a "Yes" decision to buy.

So, our network marketing company partners with us and says, "We will do everything. Websites, customer service, manufacturing, billing ... everything. This is our part of the agreement. Your part of the agreement as a distributor is to get people to make 'Yes' decisions to become customers."

## Breaking news.

So here it is. As network marketing distributors, our business is getting people to make "Yes" decisions to become customers.

We are in the decision-making business. We are not in the skincare, wellness, services, or travel business.

Once we understand that we have joined the decision-making business, we understand that we only get paid for "Yes" decisions.

Are you skeptical of this viewpoint that we are in the "Yes" decision business? Let's ask ourselves these questions:

- Is there a commission for us on people who almost bought our product?
- Is there a commission for us when we hand out free samples?
- Is there a commission for us for educating people about our product?
- Is there a commission for us when people see our presentation and do not buy?
- Is there a commission for us when people don't take our phone calls?
- Is there a commission for us when we work endless hours and don't get "Yes" decisions?
- Is there a commission for us when we throw skincare cream on the back of a person's neck as she is running away?
- Is there a commission for us when we invest in business cards and advertising, and drive endless miles to appointments that don't work out?
- Is there a commission for us when we make a list of 200 people that we are afraid to call?
- Is there a commission for us because we "need" it?
- Is there a commission for us when we put pictures on our vision board?
- Is there a commission for us for not approaching potential customers?
- Is there a commission for us on all the people we didn't talk to?

## The reality is this.

The only thing our network marketing companies pay us for is the only thing they want us to do ... and that is to get "Yes" decisions.

Once we know which business we are in (the business of getting "Yes" decisions), then the rest of this book will be easy. We will focus on what is important: getting "Yes" decisions.

I am sure we all sell wonderful products. But no matter how wonderful our products are, if customers don't buy them, we don't get paid.

If we want our wonderful products to help people, we have to get people to buy our wonderful products.

## Start our new career now.

Let's move forward to Mindset #2, to remove any hesitation that we have about selling. We don't want negative internal thoughts about selling to hold us back.

# MINDSET #2:
# HOW TO INSTANTLY GET RID OF OUR FEAR OF SELLING.

Does selling make us feel a little weird? Do our friends hate it when we tell them that we are trying to make money off them? Do we feel embarrassed when people are skeptical of our claims? Do we feel like we are imposing our solutions on people who don't want to buy?

Yes, it can get worse than this, but let's fix this problem.

By simply changing how we think, we can instantly get rid of our fear of selling and all of the negative feedback that comes with it.

Stop looking at selling as a win-lose encounter, a life-or-death battle, or a winner-take-all competition.

Instead, let's look at our business differently. Let's say to ourselves:

## "My job is to offer one more option for people's lives."

That's it. We don't know what is happening in their lives. We don't know if today is a good day, or if today was filled with drama. It is up to the people we contact to decide if our product option could help them now, in the future, or never.

Now we don't have to sell. We don't have to convince. And we don't have to make our listeners uncomfortable.

With this new viewpoint about our role in adding one more option to our potential customer's life, we won't suffer rejection or bad feelings. Now we can share our products and services with no stress or agenda. Having an agenda scares people and creates a wall of resistance.

This new type of thinking takes the pressure off our contacts as well.

There is nothing for them to reject. We won't be telling them what to do, or trying to make decisions for them. We will be adding value to their lives. How? By giving them one more option that they can choose now, in the future, or never.

So the next time we talk to someone about our products, and we feel a bit of pushback or resistance, we can say this: "You have a lot of choices in your life. Let me add one more option. Then you will have an additional choice when the time comes to solve your problem."

Now, that is polite.

# MINDSET #3: MANY PEOPLE ALREADY WANT WHAT WE SELL.

What if we step back and think, "Almost everyone wants the benefits of our products. We don't have to convince people that they need our products. All we have to do is **stop** talking potential customers out of wanting our products."

Interesting, isn't it?

Think about it. People already want what we offer.

Let's say we offer health products. Well, do people want to live happier, more energetic lives? Or do they want to feel miserable all the time? Yes, they already want what we offer.

Maybe we offer younger-looking skin. Well, do people want to look younger and more radiant? Or do they want to look old and wrinkled?

Or maybe we offer discounted travel. Well, do people want to travel at wholesale rates and save money? Or do they want to continue paying full retail prices and have less money for shopping when they arrive at their destinations?

Do we offer less expensive utilities? Well, do people want to save money on their utility bills and use the money for a few more luxuries in their lives? Or do they want to continue paying a higher price for their utilities?

It's true. Our potential customers are already interested. Our job is not to convince them; our job is to avoid talking them out of wanting our products.

**Instead of becoming a salesman, we have to become the un-salesman.**

Now that is a refreshing thought. No stress. No convincing. Just an honest conversation with people who want what we have to offer.

# MINDSET #4:
# SHY? WELCOME TO THE CLUB.

Fearful of talking to strangers? Afraid of what people might say?

This is normal because we have ... feelings. Everyone hates rejection and being judged by other people.

Our inner fear of talking to people grows when we have an agenda or something to sell. To reduce our inner fear, we'll use what we have learned so far.

1. We consider selling as adding one more option to people's lives.

2. Our conversations with potential customers are not a "win-lose" battle. We are simply transferring the message in our heads to theirs.

3. Many people already want what we have to offer. ´

## Feeling better?

What happens when we talk to people when we are not looking for customers? The conversation is easy. Why?

Because we don't have an agenda and we are not trying to sell.

This type of conversation is easy. We are relaxed. We are giving. We are helping. We are interested in people and it just feels normal.

The opposite happens when we have an agenda and try to convince people to buy our products. We feel fearful inside. Why?

Because we don't have their best interests at heart. We are thinking more about our agenda than thinking about helping them.

Here's a tip: When we visit with someone who might become a customer, we build trust and rapport by asking questions. Introverts are great at this.

## The introvert advantage.

Here is one reason we don't get new customers easily.

Margaret Miller said: "Most conversations are simply monologues delivered in the presence of a witness."

Ouch.

But it is true. Most people are either speaking, or waiting for their chance to say what is on their minds. They can't possibly be listening to us. They are trying to think of what to say ... when we shut up and give them a chance to talk again.

So think about it. When we are speaking, no one is listening.

What is the point of speaking if no one hears us?

# Who do people like most?
# Talkers or listeners?

Introverts rock! They seldom interrupt conversations. They listen quietly as people talk and talk and talk.

People love introverts. Finally, someone who will listen to them!

*Listen to*

The purpose of business is to solve problems. And how are we going to know which problems our customers have unless we listen?

Most people will buy from us if they feel that we understand their problems. Listeners have an advantage. Talkers who present endless facts, features and benefits? They miss the big picture. They can't possibly know or understand the problems the prospective customer has, because they were talking the whole time!

# 4 ways to become a better listener
# right now.

1.  Whenever we are interrupted, we should stop talking. No use talking if no one is listening.

2.  If our listeners look like they want to talk, we should stop talking. They can't be listening if they are trying to figure out what they want to say next.

3.  Stop talking AT potential customers. Instead, talk WITH potential customers. We should be having a conversation about their problems. We don't want to be giving a one-sided lecture about all the great features of our products.

4. Do what introverts do. Ask lots of questions so people can talk. This gives us a chance to understand their problems.

## But introverts have one big disadvantage.

They don't have enough people to talk to. Let's fix that now.

How? Meet new people in person ... with no agenda! Just be interested in them. We will build a huge group of new friends and acquaintances. Then, when appropriate, we can tell them about our products.

These people will be real friends, not "conditional" friends. We are not making new friends only for the chance to sell them something. We are making new friends simply to have new friends.

Will some new friends ask us about our products, or give us permission to talk about them? Sure. But that is not a requirement for them to be our friends. No one wants to be a "conditional" friend that is dropped because he didn't qualify as a customer. That is a bad and selfish agenda on our part.

## Meeting new people.

New people are everywhere, but what kind of people should we be looking for? People who want to move forward in their lives? Or people who are content, with no motivation for change?

We will find that people who want to move forward in their lives are more fun, more open-minded, and make great friends.

Here are a few suggestions on where and how to meet

new people, even if we are shy.

1. Join Toastmasters. It's a great place to meet motivated people. As a bonus, the public speaking skills we will learn will help us overcome our fear of talking to people.

2. Join free networking events in our area. Meeting in person is always popular. Humans are wired for connecting with others. Everyone passes out their business cards, but we will be smart. Instead of meeting and collecting business cards from 40 people, we will build new relationships with two or three people at each event. We want friends, not business cards.

3. Attend free educational workshops and classes. Make friends among those attending. They want to move forward in their lives.

4. Join an inexpensive health club. Work out, get in shape. Meet other people who want to do the same.

5. Join the 5K fun runs. These people enjoy the social contact with like-minded people.

6. Borrow a dog. Take the dog for a walk. Meet and bond with other dog owners. And as an added bonus, we get exercise. (Babies are even better conversation-starters with strangers, but babies are harder to borrow.)

7. Have a short message chat with a new friend on social media. We might find that we have a lot in common.

8. Accept an invitation to a party or event. Start small

by attending and standing against the wall. As we feel more confident, we can talk to the other shy people next to us on the wall.

9. Pick up a new hobby. We could learn to camp, sail a boat, or even learn a new language.

10. Check out the "Fun Things To Do This Weekend" list in your local paper or online. All of these activities attract people.

11. Attend a free or low-cost evening class on business or salesmanship.

## Got the idea?

We need to ask ourselves the right question. Instead of asking ourselves, "Why can't I meet new people?" ... let's ask ourselves, "How can I meet new people?" Everyone can find at least one way of meeting new people that is comfortable.

We are just beginning, and with a little time, we will have many new friends. Some will become customers, some won't. Some will refer us to others who want our products, some won't.

But the great news is that they will all be friends!

So we shouldn't feel bad if we are shy and don't have a lot of influence with people ... yet.

Meet people. Try to be helpful. In time, we will have a huge list of people who respect us.

## The worst and the best.

The worst that can happen is that we end up with a lot of great friends.

The best that can happen is that meeting people becomes more comfortable and natural for us. We will realize that most people are shy also. They appreciate that we took the first step. So go out and mingle, have fun, learn new things, meet new friends ... and see what happens over the next 30 days.

# FINDING PEOPLE WHO WANT TO BUY.

Instead of trying to sell to everyone, let's find people who want our products. It is easy to take an order from someone who wants our products. It is hard to sell to someone who isn't interested.

## Want some examples of how distributors find better customers for their products?

- "I find my best customers for my diet products at health clubs, not donut shops. Even though the health club prospects are fit, they still want my products. They are concerned about staying thin, and are willing to do something about it."

- "I find my best customers for my skincare at the beach. When I see people put on loads of sun protection, I know these people want to take care of their skin."

- "When someone at the checkout counter uses coupons to save a little extra money, I know they will love saving an extra $30 or $40 a month on their utilities. They just stand out as practical people who want to pay less."

- "I give everyone a $5-off gift certificate. I tell them to give them away to everyone they know. When someone calls me to redeem their certificate, I know they want my products."

## Look for people with problems.

When people say they have a problem, say this:

"Do you want to do something about it?"

There are two possible answers.

1. "Yes."

Easy. Now we can offer our solution. These people want what we have to offer.

2. "No."

People seldom say, "No." Instead, they list their excuses, issues, doubts, they change the subject, and well, we don't have to deal with these responses. Simply move on.

I like asking this question: "Do you want to do something about it?"

It makes sales presentations rejection-free as we only talk to the people who say, "Yes."

## Consider this.

If people don't have a problem, then we don't have a solution. We are just irritating salespeople pushing our agendas.

Sales is problem-solving, not solution-pushing.

This forces us to ask more questions and listen more closely. People love it.

The only reason people give us their money is because they have a problem, and they believe we understand their problem and can solve it!

# AFRAID TO TALK ABOUT YOUR PRODUCTS?

Some of our contacts can be intimidating. For other contacts, we don't want to ruin our relationships with them by imposing on our friendships. We talk to ourselves and focus on a potentially bad experience. Some examples:

"Call my aunt? She is so intimidating. She is a lawyer and always questions whatever I say."

"How can I talk to my friend John? He told me 'No' last time. He wouldn't even listen to what I had to offer."

"Sure, I can talk to my cousin. But she will think that I am just trying to make money off of her. I don't want to ruin our relationship."

"I barely know my neighbor. How can I talk to her without feeling like a salesman?"

"I believe in my product, but I am not comfortable trying to get people to buy it."

"I am too shy. I don't want to be a pushy salesperson."

"The tension builds the longer I talk about my product. How can I get my friend to relax so that he can listen with an open mind?"

## Do these thoughts sound familiar?

Well, now we can relax. We are not the only people to have these thoughts. Many others do.

Thoughts like these keep us from talking to people. That's not good. So let's replace these thoughts with a new point of view.

If we could relax and talk to anyone, even the most intimidating person, wouldn't that make selling our product easier and more enjoyable? Here is a solution.

While on a direct selling cruise, I listened to James MacNeil, the Verbal Aikido guy. He told the story of how some powerful CEOs were reluctant to call their friends to support a fundraising event. It seems even the most powerful people can have low self-confidence when calling and asking for support. We are not alone with our fears.

James proposed to the CEOs to be honest when they called their friends. He instructed the CEOs to call their friends and say:

"It's okay if you would like to support the fundraising event ... or not. I just didn't want you to think that you were left out or wouldn't be welcomed to participate in our event."

This simple technique took the pressure off their friends and made the calls enjoyable.

So how about a practical little formula for our use?

## The comfortable/uncomfortable solution.

We can adjust James' words and use our own words. Here is a good template to start.

Simply remember two words: Comfortable and uncomfortable. This makes it an easy-to-remember formula. Here are some examples:

- "I am totally comfortable with your decision to look at my skincare program or not. I was just uncomfortable with not letting you know that you could try some samples if you like."

- "I am totally comfortable with your decision to try our breakfast diet protein shake or not. I was just uncomfortable with not letting you know that I lost 15 pounds just by drinking this for breakfast."

- "I am totally comfortable with your decision to keep your current electricity provider or not. I was just uncomfortable with not letting you know that I would be happy to review your bill, and see if I could save you even more money."

- "I am totally comfortable with your decision to continue taking your holidays at your mother-in-law's apartment or not. But I was uncomfortable with not letting you know that next year you could take a five-star holiday with your family for less than the regular price of a hotel room."

- "I am totally comfortable with your decision to use natural cleaning products in your home or not. But I was uncomfortable with not letting you know that I can provide natural cleaning products that you could use to help save our environment."

- "I am totally comfortable with your decision to try our 'Stay-On' lipstick or not. But I was uncomfortable with not letting you know that we can have lipstick that doesn't smudge glasses or rub off on clothing."

- "I am totally comfortable with your decision to use our water filter in your home or not. I was just uncomfortable with not letting you know that you could save a lot of money by not buying bottled water."

## Easy? Rejection-free?

Yes. With two simple sentences, we let our contacts know that we don't have an agenda. Our contacts can relax because we are not attached to their final decisions.

We feel good. The people we speak with feel good. And they now have an option to take advantage of our products.

# CODE WORDS FOR "NO!"

People are polite. They don't want to tell us "No!" to our faces. Why? Because they have to work with us every day. Or, maybe they live next door. It is socially unacceptable to say "No" in many situations.

Plus, people feel that if they say "No!" to a salesman, the salesman will continue with high-pressure objections and closing techniques. That is scary.

So they tell us "No!" in "code." This means they help us save face and avoid a direct rejection. They want to spare our feelings. Plus, code phrases mean they won't feel guilty about giving us the bad news that they aren't interested.

Here are some ways that people can tell us "No!"

- "I want to think it over."
- "Can I get back to you next week?"
- "Give me some information. Is there a brochure that I can read later?"
- "Is there a website I can go to?"
- "I don't have time to watch the video right now."
- "I have to check with my spouse first."
- "I need to clear a few things off my calendar first."
- "When will you be in the area again?"

- "Maybe if it was in a different color."
- "I don't have any cash on me."
- "I don't have a credit card."
- "The products are too expensive for me right now."
- "Do you have a business card?"

These are not objections that we have to answer. Why? Because these are not real objections. These are just ways to say, "No, I am not interested." They want us to go away or change the subject.

Why are people so scared of saying "No!" to us? Because they know salesmen give themselves pep talks every morning that go something like this:

"Just go out and get 100 'No's. Every 'No' gets you closer to a 'Yes.' You have to get at least seven 'No's from your prospects before they will say 'Yes' and give you the order."

Yes, it is pretty ugly.

My thoughts?

We should take the hint.

## For some people, it is just "not their time" to buy.

Yes, everyone should buy our products. But that would only happen in a perfect world. Now, let's talk reality.

Most people need and want what we have to offer. But, life gets in the way. Let's look at some of the reasons they may not want to buy from us today.

#1. Today is not a good day. They had a fight with their spouse in the morning. The school called to tell them their child has discipline problems. And, it is raining. Not every moment of every day is the perfect time to buy our products.

#2. Not enough money. Most people have budgets. Few people have endless supplies of extra cash to spend on our products. They have to make choices about where to spend their cash. Sometimes, we are not their first choice.

#3. People like keeping their money. They prefer keeping their money more than exchanging their money for our products. In this case, the benefits of our products seem less important to them. Time to improve our sales skills.

#4. Sometimes our contacts want to keep their problems. For example, an elderly lady might say, "My children visit me more when I pretend to be sick." If this is her true motivation, making our natural vitamins even more effective won't make a difference.

#5. We were wrong. Our product was not a good fit for them. They don't need our product.

#6. People are resistant to change. We have habits. We have long-term beliefs. And for some people, change is stressful. Unless the problem is critical, these people won't change.

#7. Some of the people we contact could have deep psychological objections. They could have learned negative programs from their parents or had a bad previous experience.

## It is not our fault.

Most of these reasons are outside of our control. So how should we feel when someone tells us they're not interested?

Well, we should not take this personally. Instead, we should remind ourselves that not every moment of every day is the perfect time for someone to buy our products.

So what should we do when someone tells us they're not interested?

Ask other people. Maybe today is someone else's time to buy.

The point of having great retailing skills is not to get sales from 100% of the people we talk to. Some people simply aren't going to buy from us now ... or maybe ever.

The point of having great retailing skills is to double or triple our positive responses.

## Then, what should we do?

Respect their decisions. Allow them the freedom to choose. These code words for "No!" are not signals that we need to close harder or apply more pressure.

These signals mean:

#1. They are not customers. They are not interested in what we sell.

Or,

#2. They are potential customers, but they hated how we described our products. That's a clue that we need to create a better sales presentation.

Or,

#3. They don't trust us and believe us. It's time to work on our communication skills.

If we respect their decisions not to buy our products, we will keep our friends. In turn, they will show us mutual respect. No bad feelings, no embarrassment, and no drama.

We want to enjoy our selling career. Let's feel good about what we do. And remember the mindset from earlier in this book? We are offering one more option for people's lives. That is it.

Now we can preserve our relationships with others.

# USING A "TINY QUESTION" FIRST.

Why do questions make our listeners scared and uncomfortable?

Imagine this scenario. I call my good friend, Mary, and say, "What are you doing Thursday night at 7 PM?"

Do you feel it? Do you sense Mary's uneasiness? Mary doesn't want to answer my question. She is afraid to commit to 7 PM as I might ask her to do something she doesn't want to do. She doesn't know where this question is leading.

Mary might be thinking, "Oh, I better not commit. If I say I am free, maybe he will ask me to commit a double homicide. Or worse yet, maybe he will invite me to a two-hour sales presentation!"

Yes, Mary will be very hesitant to answer my question.

Now, feel the difference when I let Mary know why I am asking the question. I call Mary and say, "My daughter is having her birthday party on Thursday night. Would it be okay if you came over on Thursday night at 7 PM?"

Feel the difference? Mary is now more comfortable answering the question because she knows where the conversation is going. She knows why I am asking the question.

## So how does this apply to our retailing?

First, we should give a bit more background to our contacts before asking our qualifying question. We don't want to go too fast too soon. How will we do this?

By asking a "tiny question" first. This lets our listeners know where we are going with our conversation. Our "tiny question" will make people feel more comfortable with our conversation.

Second, if our "tiny question" is not intrusive, and easy to answer, most people will say, "Yes." To build rapport and to be polite, we should start with easy questions in normal conversations. This is important. We want to stay in rapport and avoid stressing out our listener.

Now, when the people we are speaking with say "Yes" to this easy opening "tiny question," they will believe their answer. They commit to their answer and opinion. As our conversation continues, they will want to stay consistent with their opening "Yes" answer.

So if our initial question was easy, such as, "Do you like to be healthy?" - then our potential customer will be more open-minded to health options. This would be consistent with their "Yes" answer to "Do you like to be healthy?"

## Want to see how this would work?

Here are some examples.

Imagine we sell vitamins. We walk up to people and say, "Would you like to try some new vitamins?"

Well, we can imagine that most people would say, "No." They wouldn't be interested.

Now, imagine we sell vitamins and we ask this "tiny question" first. We walk up to people and say, "Do you like to take good care of your health?" Of course they would say, "Yes."

And then we would continue the conversation by asking, "Would it be okay if you tried our new vitamins for two weeks and see how good you feel?"

This time more people would say, "Yes." Why is this?

People like to be consistent. They resist change. If they commit to a position or viewpoint, they don't want to flip-flop like a politician. So if they commit to wanting good health, it seems consistent to them to be open-minded about trying some new vitamins.

Let's try a few more.

- "Do you find organic vegetables expensive? Would it be okay if you got the same nutrition in a capsule?"
- "Do your children go to school? Would it be okay if you could protect them from all the bacteria and viruses the other children bring to school?"
- "Feel tired in the mornings? Would it be okay if you could wake up feeling fresh and rested?"
- "Hate being sick? Would it be okay if you could have an efficient immune system to protect yourself?"

## Imagine we sell discounted electricity.

We approach people and say, "Would you like to save some money on your electric bill?" Most people would say, "No."

They might offer excuses such as, "We don't want to change. We are happy where we are. We are afraid it won't work out. We don't really know you."

Again we will add a "tiny question" to make our listeners more open-minded. We will ask, "Do you like saving money?" Most people will reply, "Yes."

And then we will continue our conversation by asking, "Would it be okay if I saved you some money on your electric bill?" To remain consistent with their previous answer, more people will say, "Yes."

## What if we sell skincare?

We could ask people, "Would you like to try some new skincare?" Again, most people would respond, "No."

Let's add this "tiny question" again. Now we approach the same group of people and ask this question first:

"Do you like to take good care of your skin?" Of course most people would reply, "Yes."

And then we say, "Would it be okay if you use our new skincare for one week and see what a difference it could make?" We can now expect more people to accept our offer.

Want some more examples?

- "Do you hate how the sun damages our skin? Would it be okay if you tried our moisturizer with built-in sunscreen?"

- "Do you like looking young? Would it be okay if you could keep wrinkles away an extra 15 years?"

- "Do you hate age spots? Would it be okay if you tried our age spot removal cream for 30 days and see how much difference it would make?"

## If we sell diet products:

- "Do you like to stay in shape? Would it be okay if you enjoyed our breakfast shake every morning to help you stay in shape?"
- "Do you find it hard to find time to exercise? Would it be okay if you could lose weight without exercising?"
- "Hate feeling hungry? Would it be okay if you could diet but never feel hungry again?"
- "Hate yo-yo diets? Would it be okay if you could lose weight one time, and keep it off forever?"
- "Do you love snacks? Would it be okay if you could lose weight by snacking?"
- "Hate sucking meals through a straw? Would it be okay if you could lose weight, and never have to drink another diet shake again?"
- "Do you like pizza? Would it be okay if you could lose weight but still have pizza?"
- "Too busy to diet? Would it be okay if you could lose weight just by changing what you have for breakfast?"
- "Hate dieting? Would it be okay if you could lose weight, but still eat your favorite food?"

### If we sell insurance or financial products:

- "Worry about retirement? Would it be okay if you could increase your pension payments without asking the boss?"

- "Hate risky investments? Would it be okay if you had professional advisors who would protect you from big risks?"

### Do we see a trend?

Adding a "tiny question" could double or triple our results. This isn't hard to do. What we need to do is think hard about our opening "tiny question." This extra question can help us sell more products or services.

Here are some more examples of "tiny questions" for different products to help stimulate our creativity.

### If we sell a travel membership:

- "Do you like to save money when you travel? Would it be okay if you used our travel services to save you money every time you travel?"

### If we sell cosmetics:

- "Do you like lipstick? Would it be okay if you try our 'Stay-On' Lipstick and see how many compliments you get?"

- "Do you enjoy looking great every time you leave your home? Would it be okay if you tried this new organic makeup?"

- "Do you use lipstick? Would it be okay if your lipstick stayed on your lips instead of rubbing off?"

- "Do you like having long eyelashes? Would it be okay if you could have great-looking eyelashes without pasting them on?"

### If we sell organic cleaning products:

- "Are you concerned about the environment? Would it be okay if you tried our new natural and organic cleaning product for one month?"

- "Like keeping your home safe? Would it be okay if you used our safe, natural cleaning products that are chemical-free?"

### If we sell natural toothpaste:

- "Do your children brush their teeth? Would it be okay if your family tried this new, natural, chemical-free toothpaste?"

### If we sell energy products:

- "Don't you hate feeling tired? Would it be okay if you tried this new energy product?"

- "Do you work out? Would it be okay if you had more energy during your workouts?"

- "Get tired around mid-afternoon? Would it be okay if you had energy all afternoon and evening?"

### If we sell haircare products:

- "Do you like taking good care of your hair? Would it be okay if you tried this new replenishing shampoo and conditioner?"

## One more key element.

Did you notice something? After our initial "tiny question," we started our next question with these five words: "Would it be okay if ...?"

Those five words make it easier for people to say "Yes." In fact, it is almost automatic. Our subconscious prompts us to say "Yes" just by hearing those five words.

Weird? Strange?

Yes. But this is just how our minds work. We increase our chances of success by saying, "Would it be okay if ...?"

So try this for yourself. After your opening "tiny question," immediately start your second question with those five magic words. "Would it be okay if ...?"

Your next words will come easily. This is a great way to make these "tiny questions" work for you.

## What is the hardest part of a sales conversation?

The beginning?

The middle?

The end?

We know the answer.

The beginning is the hardest. In the beginning our potential customers are skeptical, fearful, cautious, cold, and unwilling to commit to anything.

But what happens when we open with a "tiny question" and follow up with a "Would it be okay if" question?

We leap across all the barriers in our listeners' minds! As a result, the potential customer is asking, "So how does that work?"

Now we are in a high-quality conversation with people who want what we offer.

# WHAT CAN WE SAY NEXT?

By using our "tiny question" or other opening options, we have people who now want to know more. This is good. So what should we say to continue the conversation? Remember, we want this to be a conversation, not a sales presentation.

Nobody wants to buy anything unless it solves a problem. But what problems do people want to solve?

- Image problems.
- Weight problems.
- Oily skin problems.
- Big utility bill problems.
- Lack of energy problems.

Yes, people have problems. They want to solve their problems. Our products can help.

So early in our conversation, we can talk about their problems. Their problems might be their favorite subject!

So, after using "tiny questions" and the words "Would it be okay if," what happens next?

People will want to continue the conversation about their problems.

# What should we say next?

What if they ask us, "So how does that work?"

This is not the place for us to dump information. Instead, this is a chance to put our listeners at ease. We don't want to be like one of those rude salespeople they see on TV.

Let's start slow. Let's start with this phrase:

"Well, you know how ..."

This phrase is natural. We are not setting up any salesman alarms. Plus, this particular phrase does so much more.

First, when we say, "Well, you know how," our audience wants to agree with whatever we say next. They feel if they "know how" in their mind, then what we say next must be true. Just a quirk of the human mind. And sometimes we will see people nodding in agreement before we even finish our sentence!

So here are some good examples of establishing the problem by using the "Well, you know how ..." phrase.

## If we sell healthy coffee.

"Well, you know how coffee is bad for us?"

"Well, you know how most vitamins are hard to swallow?"

"Well, you know how we need more energy in the afternoons?"

"Well, you know how if we drink too much coffee, we get the jitters?"

"Well, you know how coffee can keep us awake at night?"

"Well, you know how some coffees have that acidic taste?"

After these opening statements, we will see our listener nodding or saying "Yes" in agreement. Now we have our listener's permission to continue. At this point we can continue and tell them how our healthy coffee solves these problems.

## If we sell utilities.

"Well, you know how utility bills are so high?"

"Well, you know how utility bills keep going up?"

"Well, you know how saving money is difficult?"

"Well, you know how utility companies make their rates hard to understand?"

When our potential customer agrees, we can continue. Now we will tell them how our utility plans are simpler and less expensive.

## If we sell lipstick.

"Well, you know how hard it is to find the perfect colors?"

"Well, you know how we want our lipstick to stay on our lips and not rub off throughout the day?"

"Well, you know how we always have to check our lipstick throughout the day and do touchups?"

When our contact agrees with the problem, we can continue. We could show our lipstick colors or demonstrate how our lipstick stays on longer.

## If we sell natural cleaners.

"Well, you know how we hate harmful chemicals in our homes?"

"Well, you know how we don't want harmful chemicals in our cabinets when our grandchildren visit?"

"Well, you know how we want to help the environment?"

## If we sell diet products.

"Well, you know how it is hard to lose weight when we are big-boned?"

"Well, you know how it is hard to diet when we feel hungry?"

"Well, you know how we don't have time to exercise?"

"Well, you know how we are allergic to exercise? Makes us flush and break out in a sweat?"

"Well, you know how we love the taste of donuts?"

## If we sell insurance.

"Well, you know how it is hard to budget and still afford insurance?"

"Well, you know how we all need insurance, but can't afford it?"

"Well, you know how insurance rates are so high?"

## If we sell skincare.

"Well, you know how we never want to be shy about our face?"

"Well, you know how acne is so embarrassing?"

"Well, you know how we all want our skin to look younger?"

"Well, you know how cheap skincare products make our skin look ... cheap?"

## If we sell travel.

"Well, you know how we deserve a good vacation?"

"Well, you know how we want our holiday trips to be memorable?"

"Well, you know how travel is so expensive now?"

"Well, you know how we all dream about a luxury cruise?"

## We are off to a great start!

By starting with, "Well, you know how," we get our listener's agreement. Now we are walking along the same path. No more stress. Just a natural conversation.

# TREATING HUMANS ... AS HUMANS.

No one likes to feel used. We hate it when our friends see us as a chance to earn a commission.

How would we feel if someone invited us to their home, or out for a cup of coffee, and then they gave us a sales pitch? We would feel like we were only invited so that they could sell us their products. Even if we are polite, inside our heads we would still feel "used."

So be direct. People enjoy honesty.

### Then how should we talk to our friends?

Let's look at an example of how we would introduce our products into a conversation with a friend.

Friend: "What is new with you?"

Us: "I started a part-time business that helps non-exercisers lose weight."

That is all we would have to say. Our friend now knows the benefit of our product. If our friend has an interest, he might say something like this: "So how does that work?"

Now we have permission from our friend to describe our products.

Getting permission from our friend first preserves our relationship. Simple and direct.

Now, if our friend was not interested in losing weight, he would change the subject. We could continue our conversation as friends.

That's it. One sentence. We describe our product's benefits or how we solve a problem. Then our friend can decide if he wants to know more or not.

Here are some examples of this technique. Imagine our friend asks, "What is new with you?" We want an answer that would compel our friend to say, "So how does that work?"

Here would be some possible answers:

- "I am selling a product that helps teenagers get rid of acne. Do you know anyone that could use this product?"

- "Well, you know how we all get electric bills? I found out how to make the bills smaller."

- "I now have a part-time business saving families money on their holidays. Now they can use the extra money for more entertainment and restaurants when they travel. If you know anyone I can help, let me know."

- "As you know, I used to be very tired. I tried this organic energy drink, and felt a lot better. Now I am selling it part-time. Love it."

- "I'm much happier. I hated watching my utility bills going up and up. So I figured out how to fix it."

- "A bit thinner. Lost ten pounds by changing what I ate for breakfast."

- "Feeling good. The new vitamins are working."

Can you see how someone who is interested might want to continue the conversation? These statements make it easy for the someone to ask us to continue. And these statements make it easy for the people who are not interested to say, "Oh, that's nice." And then they will change the conversation to something they find more interesting.

## Now it is our turn.

For each product we sell, we want to create a compelling answer to the question, "What is new with you?"

Our answer will feature the benefits of our products, and how they solve a problem. Alternatively, we can immediately let the listener know that we are selling the products, and are looking for people who want them. This depends on the situation.

Think hard about our answers because we will need these answers often.

## How to get people to ask us, "What is new with you?"

People have programs in their minds. One of the programs is called "manners." We get manners from our parents. Manners teach us to be polite in society.

We want more people to talk to, right? But we don't want rejection. Plus, sometimes people are hard to approach. Maybe we want to talk to a stranger in the line at the bank, but we don't know what to say. Here is one solution.

After the usual mindless chit-chat, if it seems appropriate, ask the stranger,

"What is new with you?"

The stranger gets excited. Why? The stranger thinks,

"Oh wow. I get to talk about myself. That is my favorite subject. Plus no one listens to me. My family ignores me. No one at work listens to me. And you want to listen? Incredible! So let me tell you all the things that are new with me."

Now, after about five minutes of monologue, the stranger thinks, "Whoops. I need to be polite. I should let the other person talk a bit." So what does the stranger do? The stranger asks, "And what is new with you?"

And we get a chance to say, "Well, you know how we all get electric bills? I found out how to make the bills smaller." (Or make up your own answer for your product.)

Easy.

Polite.

Instantly, our listeners decide if our answer is interesting to them or not. It is just that quick.

People are intelligent. They have common sense. And now our message is inside of their heads. They can now decide if this is something that will serve them or not.

# SOUND BITES.

Attention span? None.

Listening skills? Zero.

That describes many of the people we talk to. Unless we make the effort to be interesting, these people don't have time for us and won't hear our message.

It gets worse.

Our prospective customers also have memory problems. They won't remember all the good things we say. Some researchers report that we forget 90% of what we hear. That's pretty bad.

So if people only remember 10% of what we say, let's make that 10% count. We'll use that 10% to help our contacts make an immediate "Yes" decision to buy our products.

## How will we do this?

With sound bites, of course.

What is a sound bite? A small, bite-sized chunk of information that sticks in our brains, and gets us to take action. How?

Maybe the words are catchy. Or possibly the words trigger an emotion. But these few words are powerful and get people to make immediate decisions to buy.

Think of sound bites this way. We listen to a boring speech. Facts, more facts, boring information. We won't remember most of this data in 24 hours. However, during the speech, the speaker says something memorable such as, "My fellow Americans, ask not what your country can do for you, ask what you can do for your country."

Of course that is from John F. Kennedy's speech in 1961. Most Americans can quote that sound bite. But ask the same Americans, "Can you remember anything else from that speech?" Their answer would be, "No."

Many speeches are only remembered by a single sentence or sound bite. But sound bites don't have to be long. Think of Nike's sound bite, "Just do it!" Memorable. Just think of all the famous advertising slogans and great examples of memorable sound bites. For example:

"McDonald's is your kind of place."

"Taste that beats the others cold - Pepsi pours it on."

Alka-Seltzer: "Plop, plop, fizz, fizz."

American Express: "Don't leave home without it."

These slogans are over 30 years old! But most people who heard them so many years ago can quote them word-for-word.

But we are looking for short sound bites to help retail our products. And we want instant results. Long-term branding and being memorable is nice. However, we want sound bites that trigger instant buying decisions from the people we talk with.

## Nacho cheese.

I love Mexican food, especially nachos covered with melted cheese. While mindlessly watching late night infomercials, I barely noticed a miniature blender promotion. It chopped, mixed, juiced and did all the boring stuff blenders do.

But, then they put chunks of cheese and jalapeño peppers in the miniature blender. A quick blur of blades, ten seconds in the microwave, and presto! Instant steaming-hot, jalapeño-infused nacho cheese. I dialed in, bought the miniature blender, every attachment, the extended warranty, the works! No questions asked. I wanted my nacho cheese machine!

The next day I wondered, "What triggered that buying frenzy?" So that night I watched the commercial again. And yes, when they mentioned ten-second nacho cheese, that feeling came back: "Buy now."

Now, "ten-second nacho cheese" may not be a sound bite that works for everyone. But for Mexican food lovers, that sound bite is better than a two-hour presentation. If I sold miniature blenders, I would go table-to-table in Mexican food restaurants and say, "Ten-second nacho cheese in your home, any time you want it." I bet I could sell a lot of miniature blenders.

## Sound bites make instant sales ... and here's proof!

In 1982 I moved to Houston, TX. The water tasted like chlorine, but hey, I was in Texas, so I needed to be tough. Someone came to sell me an overpriced water filter and used all the boring sales presentation facts and figures. He said:

"Your water is full of chlorine. It doesn't taste good. It is not healthy. And your water supply is from the river that runs through all the cities upstream. Yuck!"

Good try. But not good enough for me to spend a ridiculous amount of money for an overpriced water filter.

Nothing worked. I wasn't a buyer until ...

The salesman filled a glass of water from the Houston tap water, and also filled a glass of water from his water filter. He said, "Taste the difference."

And yes, the water that went through his water filter tasted better, but not hundreds of dollars better.

And then the salesman said, "Hold both glasses up to the light and tell me what you see."

I looked at both glasses. The glass from the filtered water was clean and clear. But the glass from my sink tap had tiny things floating in it. So I asked this question:

"What are those little tiny things floating around in the water that came from my sink tap?"

The salesman answered, "Little undissolved pieces of tissue paper."

I said, "Keep the water filter hooked up to my sink. Here is my money."

Now, I don't know if those little pieces of whatever were actually tissue paper or not. However, the sound bite, "little undissolved pieces of tissue paper" caused me to make an instant decision to buy.

That is why mastering great sound bites for our business is critical.

## No sales skills needed.

One big advantage of great sound bites is that new distributors don't have to learn selling skills immediately. They can put sound bites into their conversations, and let the sound bites do the selling for them. Make sure to provide your new distributors with some sound bites for your products to help them off to a successful start.

## Ready for some sound bite examples that we can use for retailing our products?

Remember, sound bites are great for a targeted market that responds to these phrases. They won't work for everyone. We can't and shouldn't be selling products to people who don't want them.

## Let's start with skincare and cosmetics.

Here are a few small phrases that we could use in our conversations to trigger instant buying decisions.

- "Makes your skin look so good, you will never have to wear makeup again."
- "Avoid the Clown School of Makeup by using our coordinated color palettes."
- "Cheap makeup makes us look ... cheap."
- "Skin like a baby in only 14 days."
- "Makes your skin look like it did when you were 16 years old, but without the acne."
- "Feels so good that you can't stop touching your skin."

- "We call this the 'pore-reducer.'"
- "Makes your skin look so young that you won't be able to buy alcohol anymore."
- "Wrinkles so deep you can store food in them."
- "Acne-buster!"
- "Lay in bed at night listening to your skin wrinkle."
- "Keep wrinkles away an extra 15 years."
- "Wrinkle-shrinker."
- "Lipstick that stays on your lips, instead of on cups and clothing."
- "Have natural long lashes, without gluing them on."
- "Makes your skin younger every night while you sleep."
- "Double-chin remover."
- "Lose those wrinkles!"
- "You never want your face to look older than you are."
- "Facelift in a bottle."
- "One more wrinkle and I could pass for a prune."
- "Get rid of the 'tech-neck' from looking at your phone all the time."

Yes, some of these sound bites make us feel good, and some will make us feel bad. But they make us "feel," and that can trigger a decision to buy. Plus, these sound bites are memorable. Hesitant buyers will remember them day after day, until they buy.

## Nutrition products.

- "Makes you feel like you are a teenager again, but with better judgment."
- "Wake up every morning feeling like a million dollars."
- "Fall asleep at night within 7 minutes of your head touching the pillow."
- "Stress-buster."
- "Dying early is inconvenient."
- "Have so much energy that your grandchildren whine, 'Grandma, slow down. We can't keep up!'"
- "Have so much energy that when you arrive home from work, you feel like going out dancing."
- "Mindpower food."
- "Genius in a capsule."
- "Instant energy in a tablet."
- "Happiness in a bottle."
- "The nap-buster!"
- "Hemorrhoids? Never say 'Ouch!' again!"
- "If you owned a million-dollar racehorse, would you start its day with a cup of coffee and a cigarette?"
- "Concentrated salad in a capsule."
- "Fiber for pizza-lovers who hate rabbit food."
- "Detox. Like spring cleaning for your body."
- "Removes the stress from a dream-sucking vampire boss who takes little bits of our brains out every day, turning us into burned-out human zombies."

- "First symptom of heart disease: Instant death."
- "Your body comes with a lifetime guarantee."

The examples can go on and on. But let me show you two examples of how others are using sound bites with their nutrition customers.

First, one distributor had problems selling his high-priced supplements. Then, he learned to end his presentation with this phrase to his skeptical critics:

"You can save a lot of money on your supplements by just dying early."

This helped close the skeptical listeners who couldn't get their priorities straight.

Second, a 77-year-old lady from Florida told me this story. She said she was the youngest person in her Florida condominium building. All of her potential customers were much older. So her entire sales presentation was this phrase:

"Immune booster - so nothing will take you out."

## Natural cleaning products.

- "Poison-proof your house."
- "Make your house safe for your grandchildren."
- "A first step we can take to save our world."
- "Clean with nature - not chemicals."

## Weight-loss products.

- "Turns your body into a fat-burning machine."
- "Helps burn fat, even while you watch television."

- "Willpower in a capsule."
- "The ultimate fat-blocker."
- "The fat assassin."
- "Fat-busters."
- "Calorie-killers."
- "Herbal fat-burners."
- "Chocolate-flavored weight loss."
- "Power breakfast for dieters."
- "No more yo-yo diets."
- "Donut replacers."
- "Lose weight by changing your brand of coffee."
- "For when you want to 'skinny down.'"
- "Cottage-cheese thighs."
- "Pinch an inch."
- "Love handles."
- "Muffin top."
- "Fit into your skinny jeans."
- "Stop sucking your meals through a straw!"
- "Stop eating rabbit food."
- "No-more-cravings capsule."
- "Never diet again!"

### Water filters.

- "Your water is recycled. We take out other people's contributions."

- "Better than bottled water."
- "Chlorine is great for bleaching clothes, but not for our stomachs."
- "Great-tasting water for only ten cents a liter!"

## Travel.

- "A five-star holiday for the price of a Holiday Inn."
- "Stop vacationing at your mother-in-law's apartment with her 32 cats."
- "Born to travel?"
- "Send postcards from Hawaii to your co-workers."
- "Travel at wholesale prices instead of retail prices."

## Utilities.

- "Don't change your electricity. Just have them send you a lower bill."
- "We call our service the 'bill reducer.'"

## Energy drinks.

- "Lightning in a can."
- "Canned motivation."
- "Takes three tranquilizer darts just to bring you down."

## Other product ideas.

For all-natural toothpaste: "Stop putting chemicals in your children's mouths."

For all-natural shampoo: "Stop putting chemicals on your children's heads."

For custom greeting cards: "Personalized cards, instead of generic cards that show that you don't care."

Colognes and perfumes: "Woman magnet" or "man magnet."

## Got the idea?

Now it is our turn to create more sound bites for our products. Just a few words can change the retailing success for our team.

# BE SPECIFIC.

Specific marketing works better than general marketing. Let's look at the following message:

"Product X gives you more energy."

Now, let's make it more specific:

"Product X gives you non-stop energy all afternoon."

Which message speaks more effectively to a listener? The second message. Why? The more specific the message, the more personal it sounds to the listener.

We want our listeners to say, "Hey! That's me! Your product is exactly what I need for my problem."

Selling is easy when we target our market precisely. Here is an example. Suppose our marketing message was:

"The weight-loss product for people who hate to diet."

Who would we attract? We would attract ready, willing buyers. They are eager to try our weight-loss product because they hate dieting.

Let's try another example. Instead of saying:

"Our super skin moisturizer protects your face."

Let's try being more specific:

"Super skin moisturizer for ladies over 40 who want to keep wrinkles away."

Now, this marketing message limits the number of buyers. However, these people will feel super sold and super ready to buy. This message speaks to them specifically. Remember, it is easy to sell when people come to us, ready to buy.

## Let's do some "before and after" messages.

Before: "All-natural vitamins for your health."

After: "All-natural vitamins for runners."

Before: "Product X for stress relief."

After: "Product X stress relief for busy mothers."

Before: "Discount travel for your holidays."

After: "Discount family holidays that you can afford."

Before: "Diet products to help you lose weight."

After: "Diet products for people who hate to exercise."

Before: "Get a discount on your utilities."

After: "For people concerned about the environment, get this green discount on your utilities."

Before: "Great mobile phone rates."

After: "Special mobile phone rates for students."

The more exclusive we make our audience, the more they feel that our message is specific to them. Ask ourselves, "Instead of selling our product to everyone, how can we create different marketing messages that target smaller groups?"

It is easy to get lost in the advertising world. People receive advertising messages hundreds of times a day. To make our message stand out, we need to be specific.

# USE THE BIG "IF" WORD
# TO GRAB ATTENTION.

We have a great message, but no one is listening. And all we want to do is get our message inside of our listeners' heads. We know that IF they hear our message, most people will want to act on our message.

Ah, but the problem is that people are barely listening to us. Sound familiar?

Certain words instantly grab attention. "If" is one of those words. But wait! We are going to use "If" twice, and then get our listeners to make a decision. It doesn't get any better than that!

Here is the formula:

"If ..., if not ..."

Pretty simple. We will say "If" and then describe our listeners' current circumstances. Then we will continue with "If not" and give them our potential solution.

Try it. You will like it. Here are some examples:

- "If dieting, starving, exercising, and eating bad-tasting food works for you ... great. If not, use our breakfast shake to lose those extra pounds."

- "If you are okay with your lipstick rubbing off on glasses and cups, that is fine. If not, use our 'Stay-On' lipstick and never be embarrassed again."

- "If you can tolerate rip-offs, being taken advantage of, and unaffordable attorney rates, no problem. If not, use our legal plan."

- "If the tiny wrinkles and lines that come with age are okay with you ... enjoy them. If not, use our super-hydrating night moisturizer to lose those wrinkles."

Simple messages. Summarized. Just a few words. Buyers and non-buyers sort themselves out immediately. Now people feel that the choice is up to them. No pressure - they choose.

## How about some more examples?

I love these examples because they take long sales presentations and reduce them to two sentences. In only a few seconds, our listeners hear their choices loud and clear. People have short attention spans. That is why long, boring testimonials and research reports don't work.

Let's be polite. Let's respect our listeners' time. We can enjoy our career and have fun with these easy sentences. Here are some more examples.

- "If you are okay with low energy all day long, no problem. If not, take our vitamins for 30 days and see how good you can feel."

- "If you wake up feeling tired after sleeping, and that seems normal, okay. If not, try our '30 days to a New You' supplement package and see the difference in your mornings."

- "If growing older and slower is your plan, relax and enjoy. If not, try our superfood supplement and see how you can feel young again."

- "If cheap, boring vacations once a year are okay with the family, great. If not, use our time-share rental finder and get a luxury vacation for the same price as a cheap hotel."

- "If you have time to sort through and pay multiple utility bills, no problem. If not, let us put everything on one bill, and save you some money too."

- "If sending your children to school unprotected from viruses is acceptable, no problem. If not, give your children a super dose of our antioxidants first thing every morning."

- "If using chemical cleaners is okay with you, no problem. If not, use our natural cleaners and help us protect our environment."

- "If putting chemicals inside your children's mouths twice a day when they brush their teeth is okay with you, great. If not, switch to our new all-natural toothpaste."

- "If you are resigned to high electricity prices, that is okay. If not, let's do something with your bill now to make it smaller."

- "If paying for those overpriced and over-advertised fragrances seems okay, no problem. If not, try these concentrated fragrances to get better value for your money."

- "If sending a generic thank-you card feels special to you, no problem. If not, send a personalized thank-you card for half the price."

- "If you are okay with hunger and nagging donut-fantasies every morning, great. If not, try our high-protein breakfast shake and feel satisfied until lunch."

- "If you fall asleep every night at 7 PM, and it is not embarrassing, great. If not, rebuild your body with our super supplements."

- "If looking out a car window or sitting on a hot beach is your type of family holiday, no problem. If not, check out our 'family memories' luxury vacations."

- "If dull-looking hair fits your image, okay. If not, use our super conditioning cream to make your hair look 20 years younger."

- "If locking the door before the grandchildren visit feels natural, no problem. If not, drink our berry-flavored instant energy drink when you hear them arrive."

- "If your present diet works for you, great. If not, reset your body's metabolism one time, and keep fat off forever with our diet system."

- "If you have time to stare at the mirror and apply makeup for 20 minutes every day, great. If not, use our matching color palette technique to save you time."

- "If paying high phone rates doesn't bother you, keep your service. If not, let me put you on a quality phone plan for less."

- "If you are okay with phony-looking paste-on eyelashes, great. If not, make your natural eyelashes look awesome with our fortifying mascara."

- "If drinking unfiltered water is acceptable to your family, okay. If not, install our low-cost water filter system now."

Ready to use this formula? People will love the simplicity and the easy-to-understand choices. We will love sorting out our prospective customers quickly in a way that is polite and rejection-free.

# WORDS THAT KILL.

We don't want our potential customers to activate their salesman alarms. When we look like salesmen, act like salesmen, and talk like salesmen, they immediately set up barriers.

Not only do they activate their salesman alarms, they also do the following:

- Start feeling negative about everything we say.
- Become skeptical of our facts and benefits.
- Feel like everything we say is too good to be true.
- Feel that we have an agenda just to sell them something.
- Fear that we are just trying to make money off of them.
- Remember that their parents told them that salesmen will always lie to them.
- Want to close down mentally and protect their money.
- Begin to feel that we are untrustworthy.
- Get scared because they don't want to change.

Oh my, things can't get much worse. We don't want people thinking this way. We want people to have open minds so that they can hear our message. If our potential customers hear our message, they can determine if our message will serve them or not. We don't have to be salesmen, and we don't have to manipulate their decision.

All we have to do is to deliver our message in a way that gets it inside their heads. Then, they can decide if our offer will serve them or not.

Unfortunately, we do things to sabotage this plan. So, let's get started and see what we do that gets our listeners to think, "Salesman!"

## #1. We look and act like a salesman.

Imagine our granddaughter was planning to get married. We telephone our neighbors to invite them to the wedding. We say, "I want to come over to talk to you. When is a good time? I need about 30 minutes."

Our neighbors reply, "What is this about?"

We answer, "I can't tell you. I have to talk to you and show you this in person."

What are our neighbors thinking? Something smells wrong. This is not how we ordinarily talk. They feel a sales pitch approaching.

If we wanted to invite them to our granddaughter's wedding, and they asked the purpose of our visit, what would we say as normal people? Normal people would say, "I want to tell you about my granddaughter's wedding, and invite you to come."

The "mystery" approach and refusing to give details does sound weird.

But we can make this even worse.

When we arrive at our neighbor's home, we insist they watch a video of all the benefits of attending our granddaughter's wedding. Then we show them some brochures. Attempt some trial closes. Read testimonials of other people who went to weddings before. And finally, pull out a flip chart that summarizes the benefits of attending our granddaughter's wedding.

Weird? Yes!

This is not how we talk to our friends. This is not how we introduce new ideas to our friends.

Will holding a flip chart, carrying some brochures and samples, and forcing our neighbors to watch a video trigger their salesman alarms? Yes.

We can only make this worse by pressuring and forcing our neighbors to commit to attending our granddaughter's wedding.

## #2. We sound like a salesman.

Want to trigger the salesman alarm even faster? Just use "salesman words." Certain words will tell our audiences that we are selling to them, instead of delivering a message that has value. Everyone knows these words. Let's look at a few of these words now.

"Breakthrough." When we say, "I have a breakthrough product," we are finished. That is how salesmen talk. If someone uses the "breakthrough" word, we know that they are selling to us. Listen to this sentence: "Our company has developed a breakthrough product that ..." Feel the salesman alarm?

"Unique." We never say to our friends, "I attended a unique movie." Unique products and services are things that salesmen talk about.

"Endorsed and recommended by an out-of-work movie star." Hmmm. What would this movie star know about this product anyway?

"Highest quality." Gee, sounds like you are trying to sell me something expensive.

"Trademark, patented, copyrighted." Is that how we would describe a new cereal that we bought at the grocery store? I don't think so. Again, our listener is thinking, "Oh-oh. Here comes the sales pitch."

"Revolutionary." What do you feel when you hear this? "We have a revolutionary system to help you ..." Sounds like a sales pitch, right?

"Never been done before." Activate the skepticism filter.

"Game changer." Did our network marketing company invent running water, FedEx, the Internet? Probably not.

"Most awesome." Hype ... sounds like a salesman.

We could provide a lot more examples here, but you get the idea. We say things such as, "This incredible once-in-a-lifetime miracle product was personally formulated by our almost-Pulitzer-Prize-winning scientist who is part of a team that discovered something wonderful in the past."

It sounds good to us, but our listeners are shaking their heads, "No."

## #3. We only talk about our products instead of what our products can do for our customers.

To avoid sounding like salesmen, here is a principle that we should remember.

Salesmen only talk about their products. They talk about the milligrams of each component of the vitamin. They describe how this skincare product penetrates through 1,600 layers of skin. They describe the unique booking engine the travel service uses to get a discount on a hotel room.

Salesman describe **what** the product or service is.

### We don't want to sound like that.

So what should we say? How can we avoid talking about our products?

Instead of describing our products, we will describe what our products do. We will describe the experience that our listener wants.

And isn't that what they really want to hear? They don't just want our products; they want what our products can do for them.

Let's look at an example to illustrate this.

### Discounted travel.

Salesman: "When you book your travel through our online search engine, we send a request to the 32 most popular competing search engines and aggregate the results. Through our massive buying power, we negotiate the lowest commissions and rates, so that we can pass the savings on to you."

Ugh.

Yes, everything the salesman said was true. But because he merely described his wonderful product, his audience felt their salesman alarms ringing.

Now let's look at a different approach. We will simply describe the ultimate benefit to our listeners.

Us: "When you use our travel service, you arrive at your chosen hotel. When you check in, you notice that your bill is about $85 less than what you expected. So, you decide to use that savings to go out and have a nice dinner with your spouse."

Our listeners see this movie inside of their minds. They visualize taking their spouse out to a nice dinner while still staying within their vacation budget.

Is our audience sounding the salesman alarm? No. They are thinking about that dinner, a nice bottle of wine, or their favorite food.

## The difference?

In the first example, the audience resisted the salesman's offer.

In the second example, our audience visualized what our products could do for them.

Which approach do you think would be more successful?

Let's apply this concept to some products so we can practice this principle.

## Nutrition.

Salesman: "We have the exclusive rights to a proprietary formula with the main component found 300 feet below an active volcano that is mined by Tasmanian devils. Over 200 independent studies prove this is the most powerful mineral element and unique formulation known to mankind. This has never been done before ... and we are the only company that will ever have this one-of-a-kind miracle product. This is the next big thing."

Groan. We can do better.

Us: "When you take our vitamins, you won't worry about that 2 PM energy slump. Instead, you will feel like finishing your projects and work quickly. Why? So you can go home early from work and have some fun with the family. Life is so much better when we have more energy."

Potential customers care about results much more than they care about technical ingredient reports.

## Utilities.

Salesman: "With the recent deregulation of energy in this area, the potential is huge. Our company purchases electricity in bulk by monitoring the fluctuation of prices, similar to the stock market. Since the management has a combined 400 years of energy market experience, they are geniuses. The savings they create are passed on to the customers."

Yes, sounds like someone is trying to sell us something. Let's try it our way.

Us: "If you want a lower electric bill, simply fill out this quick online form with your address. Nothing will change except you will get a lower electric bill. So while your husband fills out the online form, tell me: What do you plan to do with the extra $40 you will save every month?"

## Skincare.

Salesman: "We discovered the hidden secret of anti-aging. It's like reversing the clock for your skin. Hollywood celebrities pay tens of thousands of dollars for a competing product, but our company decided to release this hidden gem to us commoners. Imagine owning a product meant for the rich and famous at a fraction of what they pay."

OK, this salesman is just a bit better, but still isn't any competition for us. We will talk to our prospective customers like real people. Let's try this.

Us: "We hate listening to our skin wrinkle while we sleep. This anti-aging cream stops wrinkles. Period. I wanted you to know that you can love our anti-aging cream, or you can love your wrinkles."

## Diet products.

Salesman: "The fastest, safest, most exciting, proprietary patented magic formula that targets the problem fat areas and turns them into muscle due to its strategic synergy of working with the metabolic computer inside your brain to retrain your mind back to the Stone Age when we were all fit."

Huh?

This salesman attended too many sales meetings. All these wonderful phrases mean something to him, but are only a blur to the rest of us.

Can we find a better way to communicate?

Us: "Take this product and go find the skinny jeans in your closet."

That is how real people talk. Direct and to the point. When we describe what our products do for our buyers, our buyers won't have to figure out if our products will serve them or not.

## Cosmetics.

Salesman: "The molecular structure of our product not only feeds your skin nutrients with its bioactive technology, it assists in communicating with your cells to create a natural tone suitable for all skin types. This assists our foundation and colors to coordinate with your natural skin pigmentation. Plus it has all 2,000 essential minerals and won an award somewhere."

Us: "Most people are afraid to look like they graduated from the Circus Clown School of Makeup. They love our coordinated colors. They will look like a million dollars every time they leave their homes."

Okay, we get the point. Instead of talking about what our product **is** (and turning on the salesman alarm) ... we will talk about what our product **does** for our customers.

## What if ...?

But what if we forget and start talking like a salesman? What if we use big words, complicated terms, and industry jargon?

It happens. The quick solution is to practice the phrase, "which means." As soon as we catch ourselves talking like a salesman, we use the words "which means" to explain what we are trying to say. Some examples.

"All-natural and organic ... which means you won't be eating any chemicals in our food bars."

"Smart rate ... which means every month we look for the lowest rate. We guarantee you will save money."

"Chelated-transfer technology ... which means our nutrients will be going IN your body, not THROUGH your body."

"Dermal absorption ionic transfer ... which means our moisturizer goes into your skin, not just on top of your skin."

## "Oh, that's why."

When we talk to someone, and they change the subject and slowly back away, now we know why. We triggered their "salesman alarm."

Maybe we started our conversation by telling them, "I am a health and wellness consultant with a life coach background, focused on helping others self-actualize their perfect wellness state with proprietary patented mind-over-matter methodologies while enhancing their mitochondrial efficiency."

This opening statement would drive anyone away!

People react to us and what we say. If everyone changes the subject or politely excuses themselves from our conversation, that is a hint. We need to change.

## And then what?

If someone asks us for more details (which means we did well with our opening statement), we want to continue talking like a normal person. That means we use ordinary words and talk about how our product benefits people.

Direct. Honest. Simple.

# PEOPLE DON'T REALLY WANT TO BUY THINGS.

They want to keep their money.

**However,** people are happy to invest in products that give them the experiences that they want.

Let's say that it costs $20 to go to the movies. We exchange our $20 for 90 minutes of entertainment. We could wait three months and watch the same movie on our television screen for less. But, we are not concerned with price. We are investing in the surround sound and big-screen experience. And the popcorn is great too.

Teenagers are happy to invest $100 for a concert experience with their favorite band. That seems like a lot of money for a few hours of entertainment. But, the memory of that concert experience can last a lifetime.

Runners will invest $300 for a pair of premium running shoes. Yes, they can buy shoes for less. But they will invest huge amounts of money into their shoes for quality, comfort, and image.

Do people invest their money into a fine wine experience? Sometimes they invest three or four times the cost of a bottle of wine to experience it at a fancy restaurant.

How about gourmet food experiences? Certainly fast food costs less. Yet most people will pay more for higher-quality food and a better dining experience. Yes, plates and silverware are better than a paper wrapper and fingers.

The local grocery store can sell bargain skincare and cosmetics. Yet many women invest in spa treatments and high-end skincare because they want a better experience.

Does everyone drive the least expensive car? Of course not. We invest in a better driving experience, or invest in a car that reflects a better image.

Do our teenagers want brand-name clothes for status among their friends, or generic clothes that cost less? If it is their parents' money, they insist on brand-name clothes.

Brand-name water commands premium prices. And yet it is just ... water!

## Experience is more important than price.

What if our listeners say this? "These products cost too much money."

What are they really saying?

They are telling us they don't see the value in our offering. It is not a matter of price, it is a matter of perceived value. They want a better experience.

Discounting the price of a product that nobody wants won't fix the problem.

If people perceive our products as boring, not useful, hard to use, etc., we need to fix those problems first.

Cost is not the issue. If cost was the issue, no one would buy luxury automobiles. No one would buy expensive jewelry. Everyone would buy the cheapest shoes available.

We buy based on value and getting the experience that we want.

## Creating value?

The first step to creating value is to talk about the final experience or the end result, not what the product is. Want some examples?

## Vacuum cleaners.

We could talk about the chainsaw-quality powerful motor. We could show graphs illustrating the suction power per square centimeter. We could show how it could vacuum up a 15-pound bowling ball. How about adding the background of the company founder, the six-year guarantee, the powerful dust-catching bag, and the backing of the Vacuum Cleaners Association?

Is that what people want to hear?

No! They want a clean home. They want their home to be free of dust particles in the air. They want their carpets to be clean so their children can crawl around.

If we sell vacuum cleaners, we should describe the final experience to our potential customers. We would describe the clean home and the feeling of safety while their children crawled on the floor.

## Nutrition.

Of course we would avoid words like breakthrough, revolutionary, unique, scientifically-proven, and proprietary. These words don't create value in the minds of our listeners, but instead, turn on the "salesman alarm." These words only describe the product.

Instead, we would describe the experience. The experience could be peace of mind by taking one tablet in the morning and feeling secure about the nutrition we're getting. Or we could describe the feeling of waking up in the morning feeling like we are 16 years old all over again, but with better judgment. How about describing the feeling of knowing that we have provided our children with the basic nutrition they need to stay healthy?

## Skincare.

Do people care about how our skincare penetrates 17,000 layers of skin? Or that we can fluff up the size of an individual cell with extra moisture? Or that our research scientists received an award from somebody, somewhere, at some time? Of course not.

What do people care about? They want to look good. To look younger. To prevent wrinkles. To lose their current wrinkles. To have their skin feel young and healthy instead of dry and withered. They want people to say to them, "Wow. Your skin looks so good and healthy." And, they want to avoid hearing people say to them, "Oh, my mistake. I thought you were her mother, not her sister."

Okay, maybe that is slightly exaggerated.

## Natural cleaning products.

What about natural cleaning products? Are people really interested in the individual ingredients? Do they want to see a video of our manufacturing process? Are they interested in reading our brochure filled with vague words such as quality, concern, respect for our environment, and purity? No!

Our prospective customers want a clean home without chemicals. They want to create an environment for their children that is free from chemical residue. They want to feel good about their contribution to Planet Earth.

## Travel services.

Do people care about our special computer technology that shops for better prices? Are they impressed that the company founder loves to travel? Do they care which consortiums or associations our company belongs to? No!

They want to hear about their future travel experience. They want to feel the excitement of getting a lower price than their neighbor. They want to dream about that special holiday with their family that they will remember forever. They want to see themselves on the way to the airport to that dream vacation of a lifetime.

Our listeners will visualize themselves taking a selfie from the top of Machu Picchu. Or laughing about their boss at work while they are sitting on a luxury cruise. They want the anticipation of that special holiday to replace the dread of spending two weeks at their mother-in-law's.

## They want to hear about their experience, not our products.

Are we starting to understand what people want? They don't want to know what we sell, or even how it works. They want to know, "If I invest my money, will I get the experience that I want?"

Cost is secondary to getting the experience they want. So when we hear complaints about the cost, that should be a reminder that we talked about the wrong things. Everyone is willing to invest more money, almost every time, to get the dream experience they desire.

# KEEPING IT SIMPLE.

Humans sometimes avoid simple solutions because we think complicated solutions are better. We don't take the time to see the obvious.

There is a popular story on the Internet that goes like this:

Sherlock Holmes and Dr. Watson went on a camping trip. As they lay down for the night, their conversation drifted to:

Holmes: "Watson, look up at the sky and tell me what you see."

Watson: "I see millions and millions of stars."

Holmes: "And what does that tell you?"

Watson: "Astronomically, it tells me that there are millions of galaxies and potentially billions of planets. Theologically, it tells me that God is great and that we are small. Meteorologically, it tells me that we will have a beautiful day tomorrow. What does it tell you?"

Holmes: "Watson, you bonehead. Somebody stole our tent."

◇◇◇◇◇

How does this apply to our lives as network marketers? Well, you know how we make things too complicated? Too much information and too many choices will ruin our chances for retail customers. They don't have time for our long presentations.

Let's look at a common example of how we make choices confusing. Imagine an anonymous nutritional company representative who is meeting a potential customer.

Sample conversation ...

"Hi Bill, how are you feeling these days?"

"Uh, not bad, my asthma gets me a bit with all the pollen in the air, and I had a bit of that bad flu that's been going around."

"Ah-ha, that is because your proanthocyanidin intake is under the recommended daily intake set down by the Australian Institute of Sport's medical team of experts for people of your height and weight and skin tone."

"What?"

"You know, the antioxidant portion of your diet is synthetically produced, and it's working against all the other nutrients that are squeezing their way through your arteriosclerosisised blood vessels and the mucosal lining of your lungs is being overwhelmed by the positively ionized dust particles that create a bronchiolar constriction which leads to shortness of breath and eventually death."

"Say it again?"

"I think you are close to dying because you obviously haven't read Doctor X's latest installment on the importance of combining resonating Vitamin 13 co-factors with the botanical extracts from the prickly pear cactus, which is cen-trifugally spun in a vacuum to produce the highest-quality free-radical-fighting, cancer-scavenging, lung-cleaning, colon-cleansing, lactobacillus-acidophilus-enriched super-food from the lake in the Blue Mountains that has been blessed by the 17 monks from the island of Owba-Owba, which is proved in the quadruple blind study that shows we are all going to die soon if we don't take the tablets I have here in my bag. Would you like to buy at retail or can I show you how to get them at wholesale?"

"Umm, I am having trouble following you. Could you explain that again for me?"

(Note: None of the above is to be taken as advice for medical issues, please. This is only an illustration.)

◇◇◇◇◇

## Overkill?

Our example is an exaggeration, but we get the point. Most people are trying too hard to become experts. They spend endless hours studying the products, researching and watching videos. But that's not what a customer cares about! They only care about their results.

Knowing the molecular structure of the ingredients of our products is not the secret success recipe for retailing.

Being able to look someone in the eye with a sincere desire to impact and better their life ... works.

The challenge is that most network marketers are too afraid to look people in the eye. So they show them graphs, and papers, and research studies.

Plain, clear, normal conversation is what our listeners want.

# HERE IS THE SHORT STORY.

Sometimes people lean back, fold their arms, and roll their eyes. They ask embarrassing questions and put up objections. Or, sometimes people are too skeptical to even listen to our presentation. These are not good signs. So what can we do?

When we get negative feedback, here is a simple phrase that helps:

## "Here is the short story."

This little phrase disarms our listeners. They feel our message will be very short, to the point, with no sales tricks or high-pressure closing techniques.

How long should our short story be?

It must be as short as possible. We only have a small window of opportunity. People won't be patient with us for very long. So the shorter we can make our story, the better.

If we plan well, we will amaze ourselves with how much we can pack into a 10- or 15-second story.

In our short story, our listeners will hear the summary of our offer. This is all they need to make up their minds. At the end of our short story, if the answer is "No," then we are done. And if they like our offer, they will ask for more information if they need it.

Remember, the short stories are summaries. We don't have to pack them full of testimonials, facts, information, data, and all the boring bits that people hate.

## Examples of short stories.

- "So here is the short story. Instead of donuts, you drink our power shake for breakfast. Now you can manage your weight for the rest of your life."

- "So here is the short story. You will lose weight by changing what you have for breakfast."

- "So here is the short story. Same electricity, smaller bill."

- "So here is the short story. You can eat five pounds of raw vegetables every day, or use our concentrated vegetable supplement capsules. Guess which option your children will want."

- "So here is the short story. Dying early is so inconvenient. We should take better care of our bodies. These supplements help guarantee that our bodies have the basic nutrition to be healthy."

- "So here is the short story. You have to pay your mobile phone bill. When you use this credit card at your local stores or on the Internet, those merchants will pay part of your mobile phone bill. So do you want to pay your entire mobile phone bill yourself? Or would you like these merchants to pay part or all of your bill for you?"

- "So here is the short story. Use our night cream every night, and you won't have to listen to your skin wrinkle while you are in bed."

- "So here is the short story. This stops your skin from wrinkling while you sleep."

- "So here is the short story. Every face will wrinkle. But we can delay those wrinkles an extra 15 years with good moisturizers."

- "So here is the short story. You can lose those tiny wrinkles, or you can keep them."

- "So here is the short story. You will wake up early, feeling like a million dollars. And, you can delete the alarm app from your smartphone."

- "So here is the short story. Yes, you have to send thank-you cards, holiday cards, anniversary cards and more. This service makes it easy ... and cheaper."

- "So here is the short story. You clean your house, scrub your shower, and do laundry. Help our environment by using our natural cleaners instead of the chemical cleaners you use now."

- "So here is the short story. Your kids brush their teeth twice a day. You and I don't like putting chemicals in our children's mouths. Use this all-natural toothpaste instead."

- "So here is the short story. You drink coffee. And you pay a fortune at the local coffee shop. This coffee is better for you, tastes better, and costs less. Not much else I can say."

- "So here is the short story. You travel. Hotels, airlines, and car rentals add up. Pay less when you book through us. Spend the money that you save on your family."

# Let's review.

#1. When we use our short story, we get a chance to put the summary of our offer inside our listeners' heads.

#2. We only have a few seconds to do this while our listeners have an open mind. So we have to be quick.

#3. The "here is the short story" phrase helps remove skepticism.

#4. And finally, this phrase gives us confidence. No matter how bad the objection or question is, we have a set answer that allows us to deliver our message. This helps remove our fear of talking to people.

## Is this the only phrase to disarm sales resistance?

No. We will find more "disarming" phrases with experience. For example, we could say this:

"I am sure you have a lot of questions, so what would you like to know first?"

Same result. Our potential customers won't feel pressured when we turn the conversation over to them.

Selling should be a pleasant experience for both parties.

# ASK OPEN-ENDED QUESTIONS.

The only reason for business to exist is to solve people's problems.

- If people lived forever, selling vitamins would be hard.
- If people never wrinkled, selling skincare would be hard.
- If people were fit, selling diet products would be hard.
- If people ... well, we get the idea.

If we do the talking, how will we know what problems people have? We would have to guess.

Is there a better way? Sure.

Instead of guessing, we should ask people to tell us their problems. People are happy to share their suffering with anyone and everyone.

This is where good listeners have the advantage. Remember the introvert advantage?

Here are some sample open-ended questions.

- "What kind of health results are you looking for?"
- "What kind of diets did you try before?"
- "What is the biggest skincare challenge you have now?"

- "Can you tell me what you think would be the perfect vacation?"
- "What didn't work out on your last vacation?"
- "Why do you like coffee so much?"

The more they talk, the more they realize that they don't want their problems. That is good for us.

## We have to solve their problems.

That means no guessing. If we guessed, we could end up telling our potential customer about our energy savings, when all he wanted was a better night's sleep!

We can't solve problems unless we know what the problems are.

# YOU HAVE TO LOVE
# GIRL SCOUT COOKIES.

For over 100 years, the Girl Scouts organization has taught girls amazing sales skills. These young girls learn:

- How to find customers.
- How to use effective opening lines.
- Follow-up techniques.
- How to ask for the sale.
- Closing.

A great marketing education for a nine-year-old girl, right?

They also learn important business skills such as:

- Not all of the money you collect is profit. Those cookies aren't free.
- A percentage of the sale goes to national and regional levels.
- And yes, a small percentage goes to the local troop.

Even better, the Girl Scouts also learn:

- Planning.
- Scheduling.
- Teamwork.

- Finance.

- Organization.

- Communication.

- And much, much more.

Instead of earning commissions, the girls receive recognition and incentive gifts.

Here are three main ways the girls sell cookies.

## Method #1: Door-to-door.

The girls walk around their neighborhood, hope people are home, hope they answer the door, and give them their sales speech. They take the neighbor's order, return a few weeks later, hope their neighbor is home, deliver the cookies and collect the money.

Effective? Yes. People feel obligated to buy Girl Scout cookies because ... someone asked them.

Many people would become our customers if we would just ask. However, we prejudge people. Sometimes our internal dialogue says, "Oh, they wouldn't be interested." So we never ask. And these people never have the opportunity to support us, or get the benefits of our products.

## But there is another secret at work here.

Many years ago, one Girl Scout sold an incredible amount of cookies. Her sales were far above the other girls' sales. Someone wanted to find out her secret and arranged an interview with her.

He asked, "So what is your secret to selling all those cookies?"

She replied, "Oh, I don't know. I don't do anything special."

He continued, "Well, you must be doing something very special. You sold more cookies than anyone else. Do you have a special sales pitch? A secret opening line?"

She replied, "No. I don't think so."

He continued, "Well, when you go up to the door, what do you say when someone answers the door?"

She replied, "Do you want to buy some Girl Scout cookies?"

He continued, "That's it? Nothing else? Well, then what do you do if they say 'No' to you?"

She replied, "Oh, if they say 'No' to me, I just ask someone else!"

And this was her secret. She just asked someone else.

So how many times has someone told us "No" and we stopped asking others? Maybe too often.

This Girl Scout knew not everyone wanted cookies today. But she also knew many people wanted cookies today. All she had to do was ask enough people to find the cookie-buyers.

## Method #2: Use your parents.

Girl Scouts reach outside of their warm market. How?

They get their parents to find new customers and help them sell. They know other people want to help and promote them, and their parents should be at the top of that list.

So the Girl Scouts give their parents the cookie order sheet to take to work. They instruct their parents to use the soft sell. The girls say,

"Ask your friends at work if they want to support your daughter in Girl Scouts. They eat cookies anyway, so why not buy some Girl Scout cookies and help make the world a better place? Who can resist that? And then tell them that they don't even have to pay now. They can order all the cookies they like for themselves and their friends. Then, they can pay me when I come to the office to deliver the cookies."

Yes, they tell their parents exactly what to say, and exactly what to do.

So how many people do we know who would support us and promote our products to others?

Well, if we were a frequent customer at the local restaurant, the staff could give a brochure about our products to some of their other customers. Or what if we actively promoted a local charity organization? Many of our co-promoters of the charity would say, "Hey, I would rather buy these products from you than from some competitor that I don't know."

People like to feel needed. They love to help others. Why not give them a chance to spread the word about our products?

## Method #3: Set up a booth or table.

Many retail stores will let Girl Scouts sell cookies outside their front door. They want to show their customers that they support local fundraising efforts.

Now, the local retail stores probably won't let us set up a table, but we can set up a display or table in many markets, fairs, and networking events.

Here is the advantage of this method. We meet new people who might want what we sell. When we create a new customer with this method, good things happen. First, this doesn't have to be a one-time sale. We have the potential to create a customer for life. Now that is a lot of residual income. Take the time to calculate how much we would earn if this new customer reorders monthly for one year, five years, or for life. Wow!

It is not the one-time sales commission that we're after. We want to create a customer for life! One good customer could "make our day."

Also, think about all the people this new customer knows. When our new customers have a great product experience, they talk. People talk about the good deals they got and their good experiences. This could lead to more customers, or even new team members.

Yes, getting outside of our warm market opens up new possibilities for our business. Exciting, isn't it?

## Here is what our little Girl Scout did.

Ella loves Girl Scouts, and she loves selling Girl Scout cookies even more. She is becoming a bit of an entrepreneur. Plus, she has mastered the art of working smarter instead of harder.

Instead of the three traditional methods, Ella used leverage to kick-start her Girl Scout cookie sales.

First, when Ella received her Girl Scout order sheet, it was only one day before our family vacation. So she emailed every contact on her list to notify them that she was "open for business." Zero cost, no door-to-door selling, quick and easy, and rejection-free.

Ella sold a few hundred boxes of cookies by notifying her contacts. Notice that she didn't sell them on the great taste or the ingredients. All she did was notify them that she was "open for business." Her contacts didn't feel pressured or sold. However, they were free to order some cookies if they wanted to support her and her troop.

Next, Ella approached our outgoing, super-social neighbor. She asked him to pass around her order sheet to his friends and co-workers everywhere. Guess what he gets to do? Yes, this gave him yet another reason to talk, and talk, and talk ... his favorite thing to do. This was a win-win situation.

Can we leverage our efforts by notifying our super-social contacts? Of course. They want new ideas and things to talk about with their friends. Why not create a win-win situation with them to promote our products?

Next, Ella thought ahead. Certainly she will be a planner in her future role as an executive. :) Here is what she did.

To stand out, she attached a simple thank-you note to her orders. Her note was handwritten and personal. Plus, she added her picture. People find it hard to throw away pictures. She created a bond with her customers.

Ella says, "They will remember me next year. Plus, I will visit them again this year if we have another troop fundraiser."

So could we do the same? It doesn't take much effort to bond with our customers. A little personalized note, a thank-you card, or remembering them on their birthday. Now it is easier to follow up and talk about additional products or get referrals.

# PRACTICE DESCRIPTIVE WORDS ...
# BEFORE WE SPEAK.

There is nothing worse than walking away from an encounter thinking, "Oh my! I should have said something better."

When is the best time to learn better words to say? After we meet a great prospect for our products? Or before we meet a great prospect for our products? The answer is obvious.

We don't have to be quick-witted or fast-thinking. Instead, we can prepare better words in advance. Still concerned?

What if we are not flamboyant or energetic? What if we don't feel outgoing and would never even use a hand gesture? No problem.

We can learn to become the most interesting person our potential customers meet.

Here is the secret.

## Relate to listeners in graphic, picturesque terms.

This is a great way to communicate by getting our listeners to see what we see. We want to move the message from our heads to their heads.

## People don't think in words. They think in pictures.

If we can present our product in a way that creates pictures in our listeners' minds, we make it easy for people to buy.

When I mention the name of a famous movie star, what do we see in our minds? Do we see the letters of the famous movie star's name slowly forming in our brains? Of course not. We see a picture of the famous movie star.

We don't think in letters or in words. We think in pictures.

## How to transfer information quickly.

If everybody we talked to knew exactly what we knew, it would be easier for them to make a "Yes" decision. All we have to do is transfer all the information inside of our brains ... to their brains.

The problem is that our listeners are not going to sit for three days while we tell them all of our experiences so they can see exactly what we see.

## But a picture is worth a thousand words!

Now, I've never tested it; it could be only 973 words.

But a picture does transfer information a thousand times faster. By using pictures, people can see what we see. And that means they will want to buy.

Are word pictures complicated, long, and difficult to express?

No. Word pictures are easy. Word pictures can take a few seconds or a few minutes. Here is an easy formula so you can create word pictures too:

## "When you use our product, here is what happens ..."

That's it. Use these words to start our first sentence. Then describe the listener using our products and enjoying the benefits.

Some examples?

### If we sold a diet product, we could say:

"When you use our diet products, here is what happens. One week from now you wake up and you start putting on your clothes and you notice - hey! These pants are baggy! You have lost an inch or two off your waist and you didn't even have to diet!"

People can see themselves trying on their pants in the morning. We have created a movie in their minds.

### If we sold skincare products, we could say:

"When you use our skincare products, here is what happens. After you rinse off our special cleanser, you feel your face with your fingertips. It will feel so smooth, like satin or silk!"

Our listeners will visualize themselves feeling their soft new skin.

### If we sold utility services, we could say:

"When you use our utility service, here is what happens. We combine your telephone bill, your electric bill, your gas bill, and your Internet bill. When you open your monthly statement, everything is there in a clear, easy-to-read format. Plus, because we only have to send you one bill, you see our 'combined bill' discount of 5% that makes your bill even lower."

## If we sold travel services, we could say:

"When you use our travel service, here is what happens. You load the mini-van for your family vacation. The children start to whine, 'Do we have to stay at Grandma's again?' So you reach into your purse and pull out the plane tickets to ... Disney World! Your children say, 'You are the best mom ever!'"

## If we sold legal services, we could say:

"When you use our legal service, here is what happens. When you go to the courthouse, you notice that you are the only one with a smile on your face. You know you have your rights protected."

## If we sold energy drinks, we could say:

"When you use our energy drink, here is what happens. You hear the grandchildren coming to visit. You rush to your refrigerator and grab a cold can of our energy drink. Ten minutes later, your mood is great and you are full of energy. After 30 minutes, your grandchildren complain, 'Grandma! Grandma! Slow down. We can't keep up!'"

## If we sold water filters, we could say:

"When you use our water filters, here is what happens. As you take a glass of water from your filter, you hold the glass up to the light and think, 'Perfect. Clean water with nothing extra added.'"

## Want some more ideas?

How about skincare? We could talk about how the leather seats in our cars show sun damage.

How about utilities? We could show that overpaying for rates is the same as burning cash. Or, say overpaying is like "tipping" the utility company on top of their already-high rates.

How about coffee? We could describe the bad feeling we have when we wait in line during the morning coffee rush hour.

## Keep our word pictures simple and listener-friendly.

This is a bad time to sound important and super-intelligent. We want our listeners to easily see the pictures inside of their minds.

Our job is to communicate as clearly as we can, so our potential customers will see exactly what we see about our products. Here is an example of a pompous "I am smart" presentation:

"Let me tell you about this unique amino acid found underneath a rock on a mossy hill in China by a team of nuclear scientists who have movie stars as partners. Our Nobel-Prize-winning scientists have patented a unique way of encapsulating this amino acid into a time-release formula that not only makes amputated body parts grow back, but it also creates world peace."

We have all heard presentations like this, haven't we? So instead of this pompous nonsense, maybe we could throw out all of our technical data, all of our pretty brochures, cancel all the three-hour presentations ... and do a better job of communicating by using a few short word pictures.

## Are these the only words we can use to introduce word pictures?

Of course not. There are many introductions we can use, and one size won't fit all. The bottom line? We want to create a picture or movie in the minds of our listeners.

Here is another great way to start a word picture story:

## I paid too much for my refrigerator, and I love it.

Ever go shopping for something and feel uninformed or hesitant?

When our refrigerator broke, I went online to get the best deal. Confusing technical details left me feeling unsure. So, I decided to go to the local appliance store.

The in-store sales representative sensed my cluelessness. He didn't set off my salesman alarm by saying the usual, "Can I help you?"

Instead, he asked what I needed. I said, "Nothing fancy. Filtered water, an ice-maker, and energy efficiency to save on electricity." Instead of showing me the cheapest model, he pointed to a more expensive refrigerator. He did this by grabbing my curiosity. He said, "Let me quickly show you something you may love." My salesman defenses were up, but my curiosity was there. What could it be?

His quick, five-sentence story made me spend more than I had planned. He said, "Let's say you finish grilling a mouthwatering steak. As you sit down, your spouse says, 'You forgot that we have dinner with our friends tonight.' Instead of feeling bad that your steak won't taste fresh tomorrow, you do this. You place your steak in this quick-freeze shelf in your freezer and it will save every juicy flavor. It will taste as fresh as when you grilled it."

Quick-freeze shelf? I need that! I don't know how it works and I rarely eat steak, but I could picture myself using this feature. So I went home with a refrigerator that cost 50% more than I wanted to spend. It turns out that to this day, I am still happy with my purchase. Just because he shared a quick, five-sentence story.

Do you have a quick story you can share about your product or service that puts your listener in the story too?

If there is a more expensive option that our prospects may love, we can say these words:

## "Let me quickly show you something you may love."

Nice words to start a word picture. And almost impossible for buyers to refuse.

## But what if I want to use real pictures?

Great. Everyone loves pictures. But here is a little secret.

Make sure we have a great caption for our picture.

The caption is the small print below the picture that describes what is going on. This is very important. Why?

Because as soon as the human eye sees a picture, it instantly goes to the caption of the picture to get an explanation about what is happening. This is the best place to put a little sales pitch about our product. And don't forget to make the caption interesting.

Here are some examples.

Below the picture of a grinning client going to the courthouse, we could write,

"Harry Miller looks forward to his day in court because he has unlimited legal representation for 83 cents a day."

Below the picture of Grandma finishing a race, we could write,

"Michael and Michelle Smith struggle to keep up with their 63-year-old grandmother who now runs marathons after adding our vitamins to her diet."

Below the picture of the lady holding up two glasses of water, we could say,

"Mary Jones checks the water from her kitchen water filter. She installed her water filter when she couldn't get the municipal water department to tell her what the floating particles were in her tap water."

### Word pictures are amazing.

We remember stories. We love stories. And stories create movies in our minds.

Forget about listing all the facts and concentrate on the stories that will create movies in the minds of our audiences.

# THE POWER OF SOCIAL PROOF.

Social proof makes buying decisions easier. Our potential customers feel better when they see that others buy and love our products.

Even if we know what we want, we still want the security of social proof. We want the assurance that we didn't make a lone, stupid decision.

As small children, we crave social proof from others. Along comes elementary school, and it is all about fitting in.

We look to see what everybody is wearing, what everybody is eating, and what toys everyone likes. If it is good enough for our peers, then it is good enough for us. Welcome to fitting in socially.

## Caribbean raw chocolate.

After a trip to the Caribbean, my daughter brought back chocolates for her elementary classmates. She thought it would be fun to have her classmates try all the different types. Dark chocolate, milk chocolate, and even ... raw Caribbean unsweetened chocolate. This raw version tasted bland and wasn't much of a treat.

Her friend Catherine was the first to try the raw, bland version of the chocolates. Her reaction? She said, "It tastes pretty good but it doesn't have much flavor. Can I have another piece?"

Then, the next three friends tried the raw, bland version of the chocolates. They all spit it out. "Yuck! This isn't chocolate!"

Guess what? Because Catherine's friends hated the taste of the raw, bland version of the chocolates, Catherine decided she didn't like the taste either!

Social proof. Catherine wanted to be in agreement with her friends. Other people's opinions affect our decisions.

## Restaurants know about social proof.

On any Friday or Saturday night, customers fill our "restaurant row" parking lots. This popular area of our city is where people find every variety of food.

A few years ago, a new steak restaurant opened on the restaurant row. They remodeled the interior, erected a new sign, repaved the parking lot and more.

Their first weekend? There were only a few cars in their parking lot. The other restaurants had full parking lots.

Their second weekend? The parking lot was half full. Still, it seemed strange for a new restaurant not to have a big crowd.

By their fourth weekend, their parking lot was full. What made the difference?

People tried the new steakhouse. Then they told a few friends. The online reviews began to accumulate, along with a few online articles.

It turned out that nobody wanted to be the first to try the new steakhouse. We don't want to take risks. We wait for someone else to try new things first.

Think about how often we look for restaurant reviews and recommendations. We want to know what everybody else thinks before we try something new.

## Still skeptical that social proof works?

**Case study #1:** We are hungry and visit the restaurant area of our city. The first restaurant is empty. Only the staff. No customers.

The second restaurant is full. People are happy, talking, and having a good time.

Which restaurant do we want to eat in? The second restaurant, of course. Lots of other people voted with their wallets that this is the better restaurant.

**Case study #2:** We go hiking in the mountains. We discover a brand-new bush species. As famous discoverers, the local newspaper takes our pictures in front of the bush. The reporter asks, "Hey! This new bush has berries on it. Do you want to be the first people to eat those berries?"

Well, we don't have any social proof, so we say, "No!" We want other people to eat those berries first. We want to see if they live. If they do, then we will try those berries.

## More social proof.

"We are #1! We are #1!" Everybody says this about their products, because it works. Customers feel secure in knowing they are getting the best value for their money. And this statement also provides the social proof they require.

Now, is our product #1? Well, it is #1 to ... somebody.

## My first trip to Las Vegas.

Upon arrival at the airport, I saw signs for every attraction. And guess what? They were all voted #1 by somebody.

- "Voted #1 buffet in Las Vegas."
- "Voted #1 by this magazine."
- "Voted #1 by this newspaper."
- "Voted #1 by this independent study."
- "The best in Las Vegas."
- "The most popular in Las Vegas."
- "The biggest in Las Vegas."
- "The best show in Las Vegas."
- "The loosest slot machines in Las Vegas."
- "The best golf in Las Vegas."
- "The best hypnotist in Las Vegas."

Turns out every tourist trap had won an award from someone.

## Think about toothpaste.

There's a common phrase:

"4 out of 5 dentists recommend ..."

We instantly think, "Well, it must be pretty good toothpaste if all those dentists recommend it." That's social proof at work.

The toothpaste companies didn't waste their time promoting ingredients, quality manufacturing techniques, or charts. They used social proof. It worked!

# Which plastic surgeon?

In Hollywood, plastic surgery is common. But do people go to the discount plastic surgeon because they have a $50 off coupon? No.

They want social proof. They want to use the plastic surgeon the movie stars use.

## When other people talk, we listen.

In social conversation, we are always looking to hear about something new or exciting. When other people have new experiences, we want to listen to their stories.

Here is an example of how a startup airline did things different. Airlines are boring. Buy a ticket, fly, and get our luggage. But by making the experience different, this airline got people talking about them.

And when people talk about things, the social proof begins.

## A small Texas startup airline.

In the early 1970s a small startup airline was born in Dallas, Texas. Instead of trying to compete with the "big boys" by being bigger, they chose to be different to stand out.

- Big airlines served fancy meals. This new airline was known as "no frills" and served only peanuts.

- Big airlines had first class and economy. They had economy only.

- Big airlines went everywhere. They chose to serve three cities in Texas.

- Big airlines had bland, corporate slogans. They chose fun slogans that were a little quirky.

- Instead of classy uniform-wearing attendants, their attendants had a fun culture of wearing khaki shorts.

- Instead of assigned seats, every passenger just walked on the plane and chose where they wanted to sit.

- Instead of high prices, their fares were low. In fact, the fares were so low they called them "Peanut Fares."

This Texas startup airline was different. They were fun to talk about with friends. Everyone had a story about their experience.

People talk. That creates even more social proof.

Everything this airline did created publicity. Publicity? Yes, that is like free advertising.

For example, a competitor sued them on a trademark dispute. Instead of spending money on lawyers, this airline's CEO challenged the competitor's CEO to an arm-wrestling contest. Winner gets the trademark.

Now, that is news!

## So what can we do to stand out and create publicity for our products?

Social proof shouldn't be the sole focus of our products' benefits, but it is important. Social proof helps remove the doubt people may have about making their initial purchase.

Let's start with this easy technique. People love joining groups. They feel safe in groups because they know others made the same decision to join.

We will start our own group of product users, and we will give the group a catchy name. Because others have already joined our group, new people will feel safe in joining the group also.

Now, our group can be formal and meet once a month. Or it can be informal, and stay in touch on social media. It doesn't matter. Groups are social proof.

What kind of catchy name can we give our group? If the name is memorable, it will be easy to spread the word about the group. Here are some examples to get us thinking creatively.

- "Hometown Losers." (Weight-loss group. Admission to the group could cost one losing lottery ticket.)
- "60 is the new 40!" (Anti-aging group.)
- "Frugal Phones." (Saves on phone bills.)
- "Gourmet Coffee Fan Club." (Coffee, of course.)
- "RV Retirees." (Travel group.)
- "Over-21 Club." (Must be at least 21 pounds overweight and impatient to join.)

Got the idea? With a little bit of thought, we can have a group name that builds social proof. That is called branding.

Plus, as the organizer of this group, we have the respect of the members. They will listen to us.

# BEFORE WE BUY ADVERTISING.

The seduction of advertising: spend money and random strangers will come to us with money to buy products. Sounds good, but it is risky.

First, our amateur-prepared advertising is in competition with advertising prepared by professionals. Those are not good odds.

Second, we can spend money on advertising and get no customers at all.

Third, even if our advertising worked, we would have to spend more money if we wanted more customers. When the advertising stops, so does the flow of customers.

## Another way?

What would happen if we invested our advertising money differently? Let's think about how we could get more sales with the same budget.

## Case study #1: Utility bills.

Imagine we spent $100 in advertising to attract 10 potential customers. That means we spent $10 for the opportunity to talk to a stranger about utility bills. Ouch.

Instead, we could use the $10 to bribe someone to talk to us. We could say, "Bring your last utility bill to the local coffee shop and we will buy you your favorite latte."

We have a nice conversation over coffee, and our potential customer can see how we can save them money. Same cost. But we have a guaranteed audience.

## Case study #2: Diet products.

Imagine we spent $100 in advertising to attract and have an actual conversation with five potential customers. We spent $20 to talk about our products to an overweight candidate with a very short attention span.

Instead, we invest the $20 differently. We say, "Overweight? Come to our all-you-can-eat buffet at Buffet Restaurant for lunch on Tuesday. I will buy your lunch and show you how you can eat AND lose weight with our Diet Power Program. Call now to reserve your seat."

Now we will have a captive audience to listen to us for an entire meal. Hopefully our audience will go back for second and third helpings from the buffet. They will listen to us longer, and have more weight to lose!

Some buffet restaurants have private banquet rooms. So if we plan for a big crowd, we can have the entire room for our group.

## Case study #3: Natural cleaning products.

Think about entrepreneurial carpet cleaners. They advertise to get new business. Many times they advertise that they will clean a room for free to highlight their great service.

We could save this carpet cleaner his entire advertising budget. How?

We tell our prospective customers, "When you buy our complete range of natural cleaning products, we will arrange to have the carpet in one of your rooms cleaned for free."

The customer wins. Free carpet cleaning for a room, and also some great natural cleaning products. The carpet cleaner wins. He gets to showcase his great service and might make a sale to clean the rest of the carpets in the house. Plus, he saves all that advertising money.

We win too. We get a happy new customer using our natural cleaning products.

## Case study #4: Fragrances, skincare, and cosmetics.

Think about entrepreneurial beauticians. They advertise to get new business. Again we can save them the advertising cost to get new customers.

When our new customers buy our fragrances, skincare, or cosmetics, we can give them a certificate for a free shampoo and blow-dry with this beautician. We could use part of our commissions to help reimburse the local beautician for her time.

Our cost to acquire these new customers? Much less than if we advertised to strangers. And our new customers enjoy the free visit to the beautician and remember us fondly.

## The bottom line?

We need to be in front of people to tell them our story. The more people that hear our story, the more retail sales we will make.

# WHERE DO I FIND MORE CUSTOMERS TO TALK TO?

**Q:** What do Mongolian prisoners, seven-year-old children and our competitors have in common?

**A:** They are not our customers!

I asked a distributor to describe his ideal customer. Why?

Because we want to know how our customer thinks. We want to sell what our customer wants. We want to bond with our customer. And we can't do this unless we know who our customer is.

Here is our conversation:

**Big Al:** Who are your customers?

**Distributor:** Everyone!

**Big Al:** Everyone?

**Distributor:** Yes, everybody is a customer for my wonderful products.

**Big Al:** Well, what about prisoners in Mongolia? Are they customers for your wonderful products?

**Distributor:** Well, no, of course not. They live in a foreign country and we haven't expanded there yet. Plus, they won't have any extra income as a prisoner in Mongolia. And they don't speak English. Gee, they couldn't even read our classy brochure. So no, I don't think Mongolian prisoners are customers for my wonderful products.

**Big Al:** So what you are saying is that everybody is a customer for your wonderful products except for Mongolian prisoners, right?

**Distributor:** Yes. Everybody else is a customer.

**Big Al:** What about somebody who is only seven years old? Is that person a customer for your wonderful products?

**Distributor:** Uh, no, of course not, because that person is only seven years old. They wouldn't understand our wonderful products. Plus, they wouldn't have any money unless they asked their parents.

**Big Al:** So, what you are saying is that everybody is a customer for your wonderful products except Mongolian prisoners and people who are seven years old, right?

**Distributor:** Right. Everybody else is a customer.

**Big Al:** Well, out of curiosity, what about competitors who don't like your wonderful products? They want to criticize your wonderful products so that their products look better.

**Distributor:** Well, of course not. They want to push their inferior products to the public. So of course they are not customers for my wonderful products.

**Big Al:** Let me understand. What you are saying is that everybody is a customer for your wonderful products except for Mongolian prisoners, people who are seven years old, and competitors who sell inferior products. Is that right?

**Distributor:** Uh, right.

**Big Al:** Well, what about ...

And so the conversation continues. After mentioning several more categories of people, the distributor finally says:

"You're right. I guess not everybody is a customer for my wonderful products. Only some people are good customers for my wonderful products. I need to identify that group."

So how about our wonderful products? If we don't know who our customers are, how can we effectively market our wonderful products to them?

## How can we know what our customers want if we don't know who our customers are?

Targeting a small group of highly-qualified candidates will make retailing easier. These people will want to become customers because they want what we have to offer.

Let's take a look at a few examples.

## Ashley markets air filters.

This is easy. Let's make a list of prospects for her products.

- People with asthma.
- People who have allergies and hay fever.
- People who can't sleep at night because of their allergies.
- People who work with smokers.
- People with pets.

- People who cook with onions and garlic.
- People who live next to a busy highway.
- People who live in cities with smog.
- People who work with sick people who sneeze and cough.

This is pretty easy. With a little creative thinking we can come up with more, but let's look at another example of marketing to a niche of highly-qualified potential customers.

## Dan sells energy products.

This is too easy. Let's make a list of people who would want what he sells.

- Computer programmers who sit all day.
- Taxi drivers.
- People working the night shift.
- Office workers with boring jobs.
- Truck drivers.
- Parents with full-time jobs.
- Joggers.
- People who work out at health clubs.
- College students.

As you can see, it is so much easier to talk to these people. They have a big problem that we can solve.

## Heather sells diet products.

Overweight people are easy to spot. Again, it is obvious that not everyone wants what Heather sells. So where should we find these overweight people?

- Donut shops.

- Large and tall men's stores.

- By the candy bar vending machines.

- Health clubs, where they are walking ever so slowly on the treadmills.

- All-you-can-eat buffets.

- Stationary people on moving walkways.

But wait, what about other people who want to lose weight? These are motivated buyers. Let's make a list.

- Brides-to-be.

- Mothers of brides-to-be. (Yes, they will be in the pictures.)

- Thin people who work out and want to stay thin.

- Fashion-conscious people who always want to look good.

## Brides-to-be? Mothers of brides-to-be? Can they be hot prospects?

Yes! In our book, *51 Ways and Places to Sponsor New Distributors: Discover Hot Prospects For Your Network Marketing Business*, we tell a story about selling to brides-to-be.

◇◇◇◇◇

While eating Mexican food with distributors from a workshop, I asked the lady across the table what she sold. She answered, "I sell diet products."

To continue the conversation, I asked, "So how is it going?"

She told me, "I am so tired. Every day I am delivering boxes and boxes of my diet products to customers all over the city. This is exhausting."

Now, I am thinking, "That is pretty incredible. She must have a secret. Maybe the diet products are a bargain or something." So I asked her, "Well, how much do these diet products cost?"

She said, "Well, the cheapest package is $350 for a month supply, but I normally sell the $600 packs."

I now think, "$600 a pack? I could buy 300 baskets of these tortilla chips for that. That is expensive for a month of diet products. How could she sell that many packs so easily?" But, I kept my composure and posture. I then asked, "So tell me. Where do you find these prospects for those expensive $600 diet packs? Let me know and maybe I could give you some advice or a tip or two."

Her reply sums up why it is important to know who our prospects are. She said:

"I go to bridal shows and talk to the brides-to-be. When I ask them if they want to lose a little weight before the wedding, they instantly say, 'Yes.' This is the big day in their life. No matter how anorexic-looking the bride-to-be is, every bride wants to lose a little more weight before their special moment.

"The average wedding costs between $20,000 and $50,000 here. The $600 diet pack isn't even a thought, it is barely a tip. So the bride-to-be orders immediately, no questions asked.

"But then the mother of the bride thinks that she wants to lose weight too. She doesn't want to look fat in those wedding pictures for the rest of eternity. She orders her pack.

"And so does the future mother-in-law. She doesn't want to be the fat one in the picture.

"And ... the bridesmaids. They already are going to look awful in those off-colored dresses they have to wear to make the bride look pretty. They don't want to look awful and fat. They order too.

"So I load up my car with as many packs as I can, and I spend the entire day delivering and talking to my new, enthusiastic customers."

◇◇◇◇◇

Needless to say, I didn't give her any advice or tips. She was doing fine with her very targeted market.

## Ed sells discounted electricity and gas.

So who are the people who want to save money?

- People who buy boring and efficient used cars.
- People who shop at discount warehouses.
- People who complain that their house taxes are too high.
- Young families with stretched budgets.
- People who shop with coupons.
- Elderly people on fixed budgets.
- People who would feel embarrassed that they were overpaying, while their neighbors got discounts.

## Janet sells cosmetics and fragrances.

Well, let's get a little creative here. Ready to look at a bigger picture?

Let's find potential customers that will spend lots of money, no questions asked.

Janet approaches men. She terrorizes them with this simple question: "Do you like to go gift shopping?" The men freeze. Their thoughts turn to standing helplessly in a department store, knowing that whatever they buy will be wrong. Most men have a big problem with shopping for gifts. They hate it. They don't know what to get. It will always be the wrong thing.

While the men are still stunned and unable to talk, Janet continues, "Would it be okay if I took care of it for you?"

Instant relief from the men's faces. Mentally they think, "Here is all my money. Relieve me of this gift-shopping torture."

Janet asks, "Who do you need to buy gifts for?"

The men might say, "Wife, girlfriend, co-worker, mom, daughter and more." That is a lot of uncomfortable shopping.

But Janet has more questions. She asks, "And how many times a year do you have to buy these gifts?"

"Oh, Christmas, their birthdays, Valentine's Day, Mother's Day, and … oh yes, our anniversary too. That seems to come around every year! Just tell me how much I should spend on each gift."

Plenty of instant sales for Janet. No price objections ever. Janet doesn't know any of the people receiving the gifts, but she can do a much better job of guessing because she knows her products and her market. She is solving a huge problem for the men.

It doesn't stop here. Janet picks up some extra cash by asking, "Do you want me to get the present gift-wrapped?" The men think, "Yes! I don't know how to wrap gifts. I would have to buy duct tape from the local hardware store, and where would I look for gift-wrapping paper? Any paper mills in town?" So for a few more dollars of profit, Janet solves their gift-wrapping problem.

Next Janet asks, "Do you want me to buy a card for your gift? I can show you where to sign the card." The men think, "Card? I need a card? I better leave this in the hands of a professional. Janet can have all my money!"

But wait! There is more! Janet says, "And you should buy a gift card also, to make sure she can get anything we missed in the gift basket." This means the gift recipient will be calling Janet to redeem her gift card. A chance for a personal conversation and more sales.

And finally, Janet says, "And I will deliver the gift basket to your office."

Why does she deliver to the office? Because every other man in the office will see the delivery and ask for her gift-shopping services. What an easy way to get more retail customers who are big spenders.

## The purpose of business is to solve problems.

Which problems does Janet solve?

First, she relieves men of a recurring stress in their lives, gift shopping.

Second, the gift recipients will be getting a gift basket they love, instead of ill-conceived gifts from men.

Janet finds new customers easily by asking men, "Do you like to go gift shopping?"

Not everyone is a prospect for what we sell. We don't want to waste our time and efforts. Instead, we can target hot prospects who are ready for what we have to offer.

## Can I target even hotter potential customers?

Yes. We do that by promoting our products to select individuals. Exclusive offers attract highly-qualified people who are eager to buy.

Think of it this way. Which offer appears better to a dieter?

Offer #1. Diet products that will help you lose weight.

Offer #2. Diet products for people who need to lose 20+ pounds.

The second offer sounds better. It sounds more attractive to people who have 20+ pounds to lose. They feel like the products are designed for people with a lot of weight to lose.

The bad news? Some people with less than 20 pounds to lose might not be interested.

The good news? People with 20+ pounds to lose will feel like our diet products are formulated just for them. Hardly any salesmanship needed.

Here are some examples of making our products more exclusive:

- Homeowners only. Special utility plans for people who own their own homes.

- Skincare for women over 55.

- Affordable legal services for small business owners only.

- Natural cleaners for people with sensitive skin and allergies.

- Coffee for people with sensitive stomachs.

- Water filters for people in the new Hometown Village.

- Antioxidants for senior citizens.

- Natural whitening toothpaste for coffee drinkers.

Our customers are everywhere. When we promote our products to a special group, qualified customers "raise their hands" and want to buy from us.

# DO YOU HAVE PERSONAL EXPERIENCE WITH THE PRODUCT?

Can we sell a product that we don't use?

Of course we can. There are a lot of reasons that we might not use the products of our company. Some examples:

- We sell solar equipment, but we don't own our home. We only rent. And we can't install solar equipment in our rented condo.

- Our company sells a product for men's hormones, but we are female.

- We sell diet products, but we are thin.

This list could go on and on.

However, the best-case scenario is always having personal experience with our products when possible.

## Okay, I have personal experience with my products. Now what?

We can tell people about our experience and they can relate to our experience. Now, we don't want to sound like a canned testimonial from an infomercial. That will lessen our credibility.

So let's create a little formula for how we will present our personal testimony about our product. We will make this formula very simple.

**Step #1:** Describe the problem we had.

**Step #2:** Describe how our product fixed that problem.

**Step #3:** Describe how we feel now without the problem.

Here are some basic examples of using this formula.

## Utilities.

I used to shop for the lowest energy rates, then switch to a different supplier every few months. It was a lot of work switching and filling out the forms, and I tried to get the best promotional rates. But the money I saved initially was canceled out by their post-promotion rates. I did a lot of work and didn't save any money.

Now I use this utility service. They guarantee a low rate, no matter what the competition does.

Today, I feel better knowing that I am always getting a great rate and saving money.

## Diet products.

I exercised, ate funny foods, and starved myself to lose weight. And as soon as I stopped this torture, the weight came back.

Then I changed what I had for breakfast. Using this breakfast shake and these supplements, I wasn't hungry until lunch. And the weight started melting off permanently.

Today, I feel great. Anyone can diet if they are not hungry.

## Skincare.

I hated going to sleep at night while listening to my skin wrinkle. I knew my skin was drying out, but my night moisturizers didn't help.

When I started using our serum and night moisturizer combination, that all changed. It sealed my natural moisture in.

Now I don't worry about my skin drying out, and I feel like I can look younger for a long, long time.

## Natural cleaning products.

I used to use generic cleaners. I knew the toxic chemical residue was not good for my family. And the chemicals are not good for our environment.

Then I switched to our all-natural and toxin-free cleaners. Even the laundry smelled better.

Now I feel great about the grandkids playing on the floor, or even opening the storage cabinets.

## Travel.

I worked hard every week for a year, so I expected a chance to take a real vacation to unwind from a year of stress. But fighting for space at the beach or hotel swimming pool made my family complain. It wasn't what I needed.

Then I discovered that we could take an all-inclusive vacation at a nice resort, for less than my normal vacations. This was a no-brainer. I jumped at the chance.

Now the family raves about how great our vacation was. And I finally got the relaxation I was looking for.

## Coffee.

Coffee? I love coffee! But coffee doesn't agree with my stomach. If I have more than one cup a day, I get heartburn.

Then I tried our healthy coffee. No heartburn. I can drink as much as I want.

I will never go back to ordinary coffee again. This coffee tastes great, and makes me feel good.

## Vitamins.

My mornings? Disaster. My head was never clear, my body ached, and I always felt like I needed more sleep. I mean, shouldn't we wake up feeling rested instead of tired?

So I made a commitment to take these vitamin packs for one month to see if they would make a difference. And yes, after five days I could feel a change. In thirty days, I was convinced.

I now feel like I am 16 years old again, but with much better judgment.

# CREATE INTEREST WITH A QUIZ.

People love to participate in a quiz. They can prove how smart they are. The questions will make them think, and now we become interesting to them.

These quizzes could be used at a trade show or even on social media or a website to attract customers.

Some examples:

If we sold nutritional products, we could create a test like this:

**Q. Which food will kill you fastest?**

A. Potato chips.

B. Ice cream.

C. Fried chicken.

D. Macaroni and cheese.

Now, people taking the quiz will want to see if they are right. A nutrition discussion starts.

**Q. Which product will create the deepest wrinkles in your skin?**

A. Oil-based moisturizers.

B. Bar soap.

C. Sunscreen.

D. Foundation.

The suspense is killing people. They need to know how to protect their skin.

Or we could make the skincare quiz more interactive. Here is an example.

1. The worst time of day to wash your face is in the _____.

2. How fast will cream moisturizers age your skin? 5 years faster? 10 years faster? 20 years faster?

3. Which foods do smart people eat to prevent flaking and dry patches on their skin?

4. Which exercise will help keep your skin looking up to 15 years younger?

5. To keep your skin soft, what should you drink every morning right before breakfast?

6. Clean, tone, moisturize. These three basic steps are from the 1960s. What is the new scientific regimen for younger-looking skin?

7. What are the two best no-cost treatments to prevent wrinkles?

Wow. Now the real skincare discussion can begin, and we will be the welcomed expert.

**Q. Which one-week holiday is the most expensive?**

A. All-inclusive Mexican resort.

B. Hawaiian cruise.

C. Florida hotel by the ocean.

D. Renting a motorhome.

People can't wait to be surprised with the correct answer.

**Q. Which of these is the worst for diets?**

A. Fruit juice.

B. Candy bars.

C. Bread.

D. Ice cream.

Your quiz participants can't help but tell you their dieting woes after this question. Here is a chance to solve their problems.

**Q. Which of these uses the most electricity?**

A. An electric iron.

B. Air conditioning.

C. Kitchen lights.

D. Television.

One more example?

**Q. Which is the best investment for saving money on your energy bill?**

A. Install solar panels.

B. Add insulation.

C. Change electricity suppliers.

D. Turn down the thermostat 10%.

A quiz is a fun way to attract interested customers.

# REMEMBER THIS?

Someone complains, "Your product is too expensive!"

If someone doesn't want our products, this is a polite way to say "No" to us.

If someone doesn't have a problem, we should focus on finding customers who do have problems that our products can solve.

But if someone doesn't feel that our product is worth the price, this is a clue for us to present our value better.

Regardless, we need to give an answer. We can't sit there in silence. So here is a reply to the objection, "Your product is too expensive!" We can say:

"Yes, our product is expensive. Our company knows that. They wanted to make a less expensive product, but then the product wouldn't work. Customers wouldn't get results. They didn't want to rip people off."

## Maybe we can't compete on price.
## But we can compete on service.

If we can create a repeat customer, it makes sense to give extraordinary service. For example, people will pay for convenience. Or, they want to do business with us because we are the "expert" they can trust.

Here are some examples to illustrate extraordinary service.

- If we sell mobile phones, we can make a house call and deliver the phone personally. Sit down with the new customer and help him program in the numbers from his address book. The competition might only ship the mobile phone along with a user manual. See the difference?

- If we sell skincare and cosmetics, offer to go shopping with the new customer for clothes, accessories, or a new look.

- If we sell air filters, arrange for a huge discount on duct cleaning for the home. Or offer a guide that explains the air pollution ratings for the city.

- If someone buys the entire line of our natural cleaners, arrange for a maid to do a thorough cleaning of the house.

- If we sell legal services, arrange for a small business accountant to help the small businessman with some tax forms.

- If we sell healthy cleaners, arrange to have antibacterial soap dispensers placed throughout the house.

- If we sell travel, maybe we can pay for their travel insurance when they book the luxury trip.

- If we sell diet products, we could include a paperback book with diet tips.

We don't have to compete with our competition on price. Instead, we can eliminate our competition with our extraordinary service. Our customers will never forget us.

# GREAT IDEAS TO ADD MORE SALES.

If we are creative, selling can be a never-ending and entertaining challenge. There are so many new ideas and campaigns that we can try. If we like trying new things, this is more fun than a video game.

## Turn a postcard into a coupon or gift certificate.

Do we have customers who haven't purchased for a while? Here is a great way to reactivate them.

Create a postcard. Instead of writing a message, make the postcard look like a coupon or a gift certificate.

We could mail this to every former customer and casual one-time buyer.

Think of the surprise when a previous customer gets a physical postcard in the mail that looks like a giant $10 gift certificate. They want to redeem their certificate, so they will call us to order. Now we have a chance to reactivate them, and possibly sell them more products to help solve their problems. Most former customers who redeem the certificate will order enough products to make this a profitable promotion.

Prepare to get flooded with phone calls.

## The $1 coupon.

Most coupons are boring. They seldom motivate buyers.

But what could be more exciting than receiving a crisp, new $1 bill?

Instead of creating a printed coupon, give our customer a crisp, new $1 bill and call it your special coupon. Here is an example for diet products.

At the end of our retail diet product presentation we say:

"Mr. Customer, that's our wonderful diet product. And I have a wonderful coupon to give you as my 'thank-you' for giving me this time. Here is a crisp, new $1 bill - your coupon.

"Now there are three ways you can use this coupon.

"First, you might decide that you don't want to lose weight. Then you might use this crisp, new $1 bill coupon to purchase your favorite candy bar or sugary treat. Well, you will gain a little weight, but at least you will enjoy using the coupon, right?

"Second, you might decide that you don't want to lose weight, but rather frame this coupon and put it on your wall. It will look nice. You can enjoy looking at this coupon, while wishing that you could lose some weight.

"Third, you might decide that you want to lose weight now. Then you could use this coupon to get our complete diet product package at preferred customer prices - saving you almost $23!

"So Mr. Customer, here is your coupon. Use it any way you wish."

We will have our listener's undivided attention.

And all it takes is a little imagination to modify this technique for our products.

## Have a sense of humor.

One restaurant increased its wine sales with a simple sticker. On the back of their wine bottles, where someone might normally expect a disclaimer, their sticker read:

"WARNING: Continued consumption of wine may lead to sophistication, cultural awareness, worldly concern, youthful ambience and POSSIBLE severe happiness."

Their customers felt much better about drinking more wine.

But exaggerated humor doesn't come naturally. So here are a few ideas to help us think creatively.

#1. Skincare products. "CAUTION: Continued use of this age-reversing skincare could mean the inability to order alcohol at public establishments without proof of age."

#2. Diet products. "Discontinue use if weight loss becomes too rapid."

#3. Vitamins. "Side effects may include youthfulness, excessive energy, and a desire to exercise."

#4. Utility bills. "Caution: Boasting to neighbors about your huge savings on your utility bill can cause jealousy and increase the risk of bodily harm."

#5. Healthy coffee. "Side effects include higher I.Q., the ability to solve crossword puzzles, and the desire to master foreign languages."

Smiling makes people more relaxed and open-minded. Great for retail sales.

## Make your offers about people - not facts.

Why? Because people are interesting, facts are not. This is a lesson for us when we present our products. Want some examples?

Which presentation do you find more interesting and effective?

A. "Our bundled utility package creates a 5% discount through our consolidated billing option."

B. "Let me tell you about the lady from Fairfield and what she did with the money she saved."

Hmmm. Not too tough of a choice, is it? Most people want to hear about the lady from Fairfield.

A. "Our Super Product has 15 more milligrams of omega fatty acids than the store brand at the discount pharmacy."

B. "Let me tell you how Michelle lost two inches off her waistline by taking our Super Product for only three days."

Okay, this one isn't very hard either. We want to know more about Michelle.

A. "A famous television show featured our Acne Reducer. It has 16 awards and trademarks."

B. "Thank goodness Mary got our Acne Reducer for her daughter. Instead of staying home from school, now she feels better about being out in public."

Yes, "B" is more interesting in all three examples because "B" is about people. We enjoy short stories about people.

So the big lesson is easy. We should talk about people ... and potential customers will listen.

If our potential customers aren't listening, we might want to change what we are talking about. Don't blame the audience.

## Business cards?

We can turn our business cards into coupons! Make the entire back of our business card a coupon that customers will want to redeem.

Our coupon can lock in our customers. Why should they pay full price to a competitor when they have a coupon for our products?

## Remember to think in terms of "notification."

It is easier to contact our warm market of friends and relatives if we look at our business this way.

Think about opening a tire store. What would you say in a message to your friends?

"I opened a tire store on Main Street. Whenever you think you might need tires, stop by. Would be happy to see you."

No pressure. No rejection. Just an announcement.

Not all of our friends need tires today. Not all of our friends can visit Main Street today. So we won't take it personally if none of our friends show up the first day.

If we opened a shoe store, we wouldn't ask our friends to come in on opening day and buy shoes. Instead, we would notify our friends that we opened our shoe store for business. And, if they ever wanted to buy shoes in the future, we could be an option.

It is the same with our products. We let our friends know, and they can let us know when the time is right for them. Remember, we are adding one more option to their lives.

## "Super Waste of Time."

We can get immediate attention with this headline: "Super Waste of Time." We hate wasting time. We have short attention spans. These words get our immediate attention.

How can we use these words to grab attention for our business?

We could say:

1. Super-slow weight loss = Super waste of time.

2. Travel shopping on the Internet = Super waste of time.

3. Using coffee for your energy = Super waste of time.

4. Buying overpriced fragrances = Super waste of time.

5. Eating raw fruits & vegetables = Super waste of time.

6. Taking expensive vitamins = Super waste of time.

7. Trying expensive moisturizers = Super waste of time.

# Referrals.

Many people we know may not be candidates for our products. We discussed all the reasons why earlier in this book. But, even though they won't be customers, they do know people who could use our products.

The secret is that we have to ask for referrals. Now, the words we choose can make a difference. Here are two ways of asking.

#1. "Do you know anybody that I can sell my products to?" This sounds selfish and our listeners develop instant amnesia.

#2. "Do you know anyone who would like to fix this problem?" This sounds more like we are helping other people. Now people will be more willing to give us referrals.

Some examples?

- "Do you know anyone who wants an extra discount on their electric bill?"

- "Do you know anyone who wants to lose weight without heavy exercising?"

- "Do you know anyone who feels tired in the morning?"

- "Do you know anyone who wants to save money on their family holidays?"

- "Do you know anyone who wants to get rid of their acne?"

Notice how these questions communicate that we are solving other people's problems? When we can solve problems, we will be popular.

## Ask for referrals early, before you present.

Here is an example of asking first:

"Most people save a lot of money on their utility bills and love our service. And, they want to make sure their friends and relatives don't overpay also. You may or may not want to save on your utility bill, but could you do me a favor? Whether you decide to save with us or not, could you at least let your friends know they could save a lot of money on their bills?"

This is an easy commitment for customers to make before we explain our details. No close needed. No pressure. Almost everyone would say "Yes" because we are not asking them to buy.

And what should we say if our customer refers his aunt?

Ask, "And what would be the best way to talk to her?"

Let's allow our customer to decide if he wants us to talk to his referrals directly, or if he feels better contacting his referrals himself.

Polite, and non-threatening.

# AND FINALLY.

Remember:

1. People have problems.

2. Our products solve problems.

3. We should feel great about that.

Selling should be fun. Remember, we are only adding one more option to people's lives.

Enjoy making retail sales in your business.

# THANK YOU.

Thank you for purchasing and reading this book. I hope you found some ideas that will work for you.

Before you go, would it be okay if I asked a small favor? Would you take just one minute and leave a short review of this book online? Your review can help others choose what they will read next. It would be greatly appreciated by many fellow readers.

I travel the world 240+ days each year.
Let me know if you want me to stop in your
area and conduct a live Big Al training.

→ **BigAlSeminars.com** ←

# FREE Big Al Training Audios

## *Magic Words for Prospecting*

plus Free eBook and the Big Al Report!

→ **BigAlBooks.com/free** ←

# MORE BIG AL BOOKS

**The Four Color Personalities for MLM**
*The Secret Language for Network Marketing*
Learn the skill to quickly recognize the four personalities and how to use magic words to translate your message.

**Ice Breakers!**
*How To Get Any Prospect To Beg You For A Presentation*
Create unlimited Ice Breakers on-demand. Your distributors will no longer be afraid of prospecting, instead, they will love prospecting.

**How To Get Instant Trust, Belief, Influence and Rapport!**
*13 Ways To Create Open Minds By Talking To The Subconscious Mind*
Learn how the pros get instant rapport and cooperation with even the coldest prospects. The #1 skill every new distributor needs.

**First Sentences for Network Marketing**
*How To Quickly Get Prospects On Your Side*
Attract more prospects and give more presentations with great first sentences that work.

**How to Follow Up With Your Network Marketing Prospects**
*Turn Not Now Into Right Now!*
Use the techniques in this book to move your prospects forward from "Not Now" to "Right Now!"

**How To Prospect, Sell And Build Your**
**Network Marketing Business With Stories**
If you want to communicate effectively, add your stories to
deliver your message.

**26 Instant Marketing Ideas**
**To Build Your Network Marketing Business**
176 pages of amazing marketing lessons and case studies
to get more prospects for your business immediately.

**How To Build Network Marketing Leaders**
*Volume One: Step-By-Step Creation Of MLM Professionals*
This book will give you the step-by-step activities to
actually create leaders.

**How To Build Network Marketing Leaders**
*Volume Two: Activities And Lessons For MLM Leaders*
You will find many ways to change people's viewpoints, to
change their beliefs, and to reprogram their actions.

# Complete list at BigAlBooks.com

# ABOUT THE AUTHORS

**Keith Schreiter** has 20+ years of experience in network marketing and MLM. He shows network marketers how to use simple systems to build a stable and growing business.

So, do you need more prospects? Do you need your prospects to commit instead of stalling? Want to know how to engage and keep your group active? If these are the types of skills you would like to master, you will enjoy his "how-to" style.

Keith speaks and trains in the U.S., Canada, and Europe.

Andrew & Lindsay Johnson
Erica Twardzik
Liz Carrillo
Kim Hawkins
Jen Barton
Tracy Beattie
Jacqui Bell
Susan Bowden
Meg Cantlin
Shawna Flanery
Lisa Damm
Tricia Horaney

Kim Sowa
Margie Gibson
Erica & Chris Leiterity
Cassie Acevedo & friend
Alaina Weatherford
Sheri Nelson
Natalie Henderson
Keri Kalebich
Carrie Kelley
Kathy Kmetz
Shaunna Kruger
Amy Kummer

**Tom "Big Al" Schreiter** has 40+ years of experience in network marketing and MLM. As the author of the original "Big Al" training books in the late '70s, he has continued to speak in over 80 countries on using the exact words and phrases to get prospects to open up their minds and say "YES."

His passion is marketing ideas, marketing campaigns, and how to speak to the subconscious mind in simplified, practical ways. He is always looking for case studies of incredible marketing campaigns that give usable lessons.

As the author of numerous audio trainings, Tom is a favorite speaker at company conventions and regional events.

Made in the USA
San Bernardino, CA
30 July 2017

# I Slept With the Bears

### By

## David H. Carpenter

ISBN: 1-4107-2586-3 (e-book)
ISBN: 1-4107-2587-1 (Paperback)

This book is printed on acid free paper.

1stBooks - rev. 05/21/03

## <u>Dedication</u>

This book is dedicated to my three granddaughters,

## Camber, Elora and Zoey Carpenter

who I hope will be able to grow up and raise, their own children in an Alaska as wild and wonderful as the one I knew.

# CONTENTS

FOREWORD.................................................................. viii
THE MOVE TO ALASKA .....................................................1
THE ACADEMY ............................................................3
ANCHORAGE TOUR .......................................................8
DELTA JUNCTION ......................................................14
KODIAK ISLAND TOUR..................................................39
PALMER TOUR ...........................................................78
HAINES TOUR............................................................136
ANCHORAGE '92 .........................................................157
RETIREMENT ............................................................170

# PHOTOS

Sitka Academy Building ........................................4

Delta Junction Patrol Vehicle............................. 36

Kodiak King Crabs............................................. 44

"Trooper" & "Tara Dawn"................................... 50

Kodiak Bear Stake-out. ...................................... 66

Kodiak Brown Bear............................................. 74

Feeding Moose Calf ........................................... 83

Department Super Cub. ...................................... 94

Yakutat Jail Cell ................................................ 97

Sandy River Cabin ........................................... 102

"The One That Got Away"................................. 119

Chilkat River Eagles......................................... 143

Haines Patrol Vessel "Challenger" ................... 147

Haines Patrol Vehicle....................................... 156

# ACKNOWLEDGMENT

I would especially like to thank my wife, Linda, for the immense amount of time and effort she put forth on the initial editing and typing of this manuscript. Also, I appreciate the incredible patience she showed with my sometimes unorthodox use of words and sentences. She was there during the twenty-five years that this book covers. She helped me keep the facts straight.

# INTRODUCTION

This book is honest and factual. Although some names have been changed, most have not. All information is as accurate as I could make it and, while some of the stories may be difficult to believe, they are all true.

"I Slept With the Bears" is intended to provide the reader with entertainment while contributing a certain amount of information. The reader will learn much about the vast wilderness that is Alaska, the animals of Alaska and the people who make living there not only bearable, but downright enjoyable.

This book was written in a personal format, as though we were communicating one on one. As you read it, please imagine me relating these incidents to you as we sit beside a cozy campfire somewhere in the Alaskan bush.

# FOREWORD

*Alaska is like every other state when you look at the bureaucracy and politics, which exist in all forms of state government. Unfortunately, the state troopers had their share of these maladies. The great majority of troopers are dedicated and very sincere in their duties, with public education and deterrence probably more important than citations and paper work. During my thirty years as a teacher in the Matanuska-Susitna Valley, and as an operator of a flight school at the old Wasilla city airport, I had many friends from the trooper ranks and I still maintain contact with them.*

*I first met Dave Carpenter when he came into my flight school one summer wanting to transition into tail-dragger and the super cub. We seemed to hit it off immediately as did our wives. Dave's sons were initially apprehensive about two school teachers visiting their home regularly, but they soon realized we were almost human. I consider Dave a sincere, dedicated trooper, who I know agonized over the harassment I put him through over the years. I took great delight in quizzing where he was working and then telling him I was going the other direction to "look for something." When I mentioned a gill net on the spreader bars of my cub's floats, I am sure he quietly checked it out. A midnight call about someone netting sticklebacks (inedible fish 2 to 4 inches long) also got his attention.*

*I feel honored to know Dave and to be able to continue our friendship. We now spend winters about 40 miles apart and visit weekly. The State of Alaska needs more troopers like Dave.*

**Richard "Dick" Williams**
*Williams Air Service*
*Wasilla, Alaska*

ARCTIC OCEAN

RUSSIA

ALASKA

CANADA

YUKON RIVER

EMMONAK

FAIRBANKS

DELTA JUNCTION

PALMER
ANCHORAGE

BERING SEA

HAINES

JUNEAU

BRISTOL BAY

YAKUTAT

KODIAK

SITKA

GULF OF ALASKA

# THE MOVE TO ALASKA

The days were warm, sunny and clear. The nights were crisp and frosty. The mountains were covered with quaking aspen and the autumn leaves made this a magical place. It was 1967 and the place was western Wyoming. The elk were active and bugling. Before this hunt was over, the eight of us would have taken six elk, eight mule deer and a cinnamon black bear. Not bad for a bunch of Michiganders who had just driven out for a two week hunt.

This was also the time that I fell in love with the mountains and realized that I wanted to live around them. Having been born and raised in the flatlands of Michigan, I had never seen a real mountain, an elk or even a mule deer. Now I had it in my blood. This was the kind of country in which I wanted to live.

After arriving home, I immediately sent letters to the Chambers of Commerce in areas of Wyoming that were of interest to me. The responses were all the same. They were always glad to see young people move out west into their communities, but unfortunately, there was no money to be made out there. I wanted to live there, but I didn't want to be stuck there, unable to make a decent living.

A little over a year later a friend of mine and I took our wives to the movie theater to see a film on "Alaska". My friend, Ron, had been to Alaska before and it wasn't long before we were both fired up about moving there.

Ron and Carol were renting their home, so they were able to move up right away. He would go up as district manager for Equitable Life Insurance Company. We had to wait until our house sold and then we were on our way. There was my wife, Linda, our two sons, Darin, age four, and Chad, age two. I was twenty-six at the time and Linda was twenty-five.

We drove up in a brand new 1969 3/4 ton Chevy pickup and a used pickup camper. We towed a large tandem-wheeled utility trailer, which contained all our belongings. We had three job leads on the other end and spent the next twelve days optimistically traveling westward and northward. It was August of 1969.

Our route took us straight west across the top of the United States to Shelby, Montana, and northwest thereafter through several Canadian National Parks and over fifteen hundred miles of the Alaska Highway. We were concerned about a nail which was imbedded in one of our trailer tires. Linda's dad had spotted it and pointed it out to us as we were leaving our driveway in Michigan. He suggested that we leave it in the tire and said it would probably get us all the way to Alaska without going flat. After twelve days of driving, we arrived in Anchorage in fine shape. Guess what! The tire with the nail was the only tire on that heavy trailer that did not go flat. Two days after we hit town and parked the trailer, we noticed that the tire had finally given up and was flatter than a fritter.

We parked our camper in Ron and Carol's backyard for a couple of weeks until we bought a house in an Anchorage subdivision called Rogers Park. Ron and Carol were living just a few blocks away in College Village. At that time, Rogers Park and College Village were on the very edge of Anchorage with only muskeg beyond.

Over the next four years my jobs would include life insurance sales, car sales, carpet sales, working as a milkman for Carnation products, and maintenance work for the Alaska State Housing Authority.

# THE ACADEMY

In October 1973, I hired on with the Department of Public Safety as an Alaska State Trooper and was sent to the 22nd Trooper Academy in Sitka.

Our class was the last to attend the old academy building on the campus of Sheldon Jackson College. A new academy building was built off campus soon afterward. Although the new building is much fancier, I feel very grateful to have been a part of the old academy with the same traditions as those back in the old days.

The academy was a worn, tired building, but heavily spit-shined and polished. The lower floor held the offices and classroom. The upper floor was strictly barracks and a latrine. As you entered the building through the main entrance, there was a mannequin on either side of the door; one was dressed in an Alaska State Trooper uniform and the other in a Canadian Mountie uniform. There was a large stairway to the upper floor and between the main entrance and the stairway on the highly polished floor was a highly regarded Alaska State Seal. It was taboo to step on it, meaning we had to walk around to get past it. Imagine how mortified our instructors were one morning when they found the Mountie in a prone position on top of a blow-up doll in a sheer negligee lying on the middle of the revered State Seal!

*****

I was lucky and ended up with a great guy for an academy roommate. His name was Chuck. There were a couple of coincidences involving Chuck and me that I'd like to relate to you now.

3

The old academy building on the campus of
Sheldon Jackson College in Sitka (Photo by author)

Back in Michigan when Linda and I were first married and living in an apartment, we had a high school-aged neighbor by the name of Chuck Rogers. We moved to build our own home in a different area and lost track of him. Several years later, when we first arrived in Anchorage, I went down to Ship Creek, which flows through Anchorage and brings king salmon in to the fishermen. Even back then it was shoulder to shoulder fishing. As a hundred or so people were casting their lines from the bank, I was watching to see if I could spot someone who seemed to know what they were doing. I planned to talk to them and try to pick up some fishing tips. I spotted one guy that looked pretty professional and contacted him. It turned out to be Chuck. He and I got together a couple of times after that with the wives and then lost track of each other again.

A few years later, as I was winging my way to Sitka on an Alaska Airlines flight to the academy, guess who was sitting across the aisle from me? Right! Chuck! When we reached the academy we learned that out of twenty-eight men, we had been slated to be roommates.

After completion of the academy, the troops were sent to various locations around the state for their first duty stations. Chuck and I were both sent to Anchorage and worked together until I transferred out three months later. I still find the entire series of coincidences incredible.

*****

The academy was four months long, but seemed more like a year. It was tough, enjoyable and educational. It was one of those things you are really glad you did, but would not want to do again. Our classes ran all day long and included topics such as operating the breathalyzer, laws of search and seizure, photography, emergency medical procedures, driving skills, firearms proficiency and pathology classes from a renowned coroner. Our evenings were spent either studying or responding to simulated emergencies. The emergencies could be anything from a messy bar fight with injured combatants to a car crash with several of the other troops playing the parts of injured occupants in a car which was upside down in a ditch.

We would get up early each morning to do our calisthenics and morning run, then a quick shower and it was time for inspection on the field. Knowing that troopers are often questioned by tourists, the instructors would shout a state-oriented quiz at us and we had to shout back the answers.

"What is the State flower?" The Forget-me-not, Sir!" "What is the State tree?" "The Sitka Spruce, Sir!" "What is the State bird?" "The Super Cub, Sir!" I don't know how Maurice got away with that answer. I guess it was because he kept a straight face and didn't crack up when he said it.

Maurice was more right than most people know when he answered that the Super Cub is the State bird. I would find that out in later years, while flying for the Department. The Super Cub is the most loved and respected aircraft in Alaska and rightly so.

We had a lot of fun while seriously preparing for our futures. We played a lot of practical jokes on each other, although the best one I have heard of was not played by our group, but by the class preceding ours. It went like this.

The latrine duty boys had the crappiest job in the academy. Fortunately, we switched duties each week. There was this ingenious little trooper, whom I worked with later on, who was on latrine duty and thought he would have some fun with the inspecting sergeant due to come through.

After his group had cleaned all the toilets, he scrubbed one toilet seat especially well. He then placed a large gob of peanut butter (chunky, I think) on the rear of the toilet seat. During the inspection there came an exclamation of surprise from the sergeant inspecting the toilet stall. "What the hell is this?" Our little pot scrubber ran over, dipped his finger in the offensive material, stuck it in his mouth and said, "Tastes like shit to me, Sir!"

*****

When putting in our applications for the Department of Public Safety, we all had a chance to apply for the "blue shirts" or the "brown shirts". The "blue shirts" were the road troopers who wore blue uniforms. The "brown shirts" were the Fish and Wildlife Protection Officers in brown uniforms who had the same authority and responsibility as the road troopers, however they concentrated their efforts on fish and game violations. Since both divisions were employed by the Department of Public Safety, they went through the same academy and received the same training. It was possible to transfer from one division to the other without any change in employment status. Some of us were going through the academy as "blue shirts", while others were going through as "brown shirts".

On February 22, 1974, twenty-two new recruits graduated from the twenty-second Trooper Academy. I was assigned Badge No. 22. My first assignment was Anchorage and I was ready.

# <u>ANCHORAGE TOUR</u>

When our class graduated from the Academy in 1974, I was assigned to my first duty station in Anchorage. The Anchorage post was a dumpy little building located across the street from and south of the big Sears store on Benson Avenue. It wasn't much to look at and has since been torn down. It served its purpose, however, which was to provide us a base of operations.

The dispatchers were located in a small dark room at the back of the building and we had very little personal contact with them. It was easy for us new road troopers to get frustrated and upset with the dispatchers for making mistakes or being slower to respond to our calls than we expected. It appeared to us, at times, that the dispatchers were not as efficient as they should be. The commander had the foresight to assign each of us rookies to the dispatch room for a few days, so we would learn what the dispatchers did for a living and with what they had to contend.

It only took me one night to fully appreciate them, but I ended up dispatching for a week anyway. I had to receive and transmit radio messages from one, two and sometimes three troopers at a time. In addition, whenever they called in a license plate number, I had to look it up on the microfiche machine and relay the information back to them. Later on, the computer would make this chore much faster. While doing the above duties, I was also answering the telephone and making calls out. It was very hectic and very demanding work.

After doing the dispatchers' job for a few days, we had a lot more patience with them and a lot of respect for their cool headedness under fire. They deserve a lot more recognition than they get. The best dispatcher I ever saw in terms of efficiency and voice control was a man by the name of Richard Carpenter (no relation). I met him in dispatch in 1974 and he was still there when I left in 1994. Over the years he became a respected friend of many a trooper.

*****

Anchorage had a small motorcycle gang that went by the name of the "Brothers". Most of them lived in Anchorage, but a few were from the Matanuska Valley, some forty miles to the north. They caused us a lot of work, but actually bothered the average citizen very little. Most of their fights and killings were among themselves, usually

9

over drugs or drug money. In later years, representatives from California's "Hell's Angels" came to Anchorage and organized the "Brothers" into the Alaska Chapter. They still carry the name "Hell's Angels" today.

*****

One of my first "major" incidents out of the Anchorage post occurred while I was driving the patrol car down the Glenn Highway north of Anchorage. A car up ahead of me swerved off the road and into the ditch. A wild-eyed man jumped out of the car and flagged me down. He was stuck in the ditch and he was frantic. His pregnant wife was in the back of the car and about to have the baby. The woman's mother was with her. Both women were screaming and the man wasn't doing much better. The baby was about to come. I radioed dispatch and was told, "An ambulance will be there in fifteen minutes!" I said, "We can't wait fifteen minutes! I'm bringing them in!"

My next ten minutes of driving would have made Mario Andretti proud. You would have thought the devil himself was chasing me. I was constantly on the radio with dispatch, advising them of how far I had made it "so far". There were constant screams coming from inside the patrol vehicle. The women in the back weren't much quieter. I don't know if they were screaming because of her pain and the horrible thing that was happening to her body or if it was because of my erratic driving. All I did know was that I was determined she was not going to have a litter of kids on my back seat and I, sure as bat guano, was not going to be a delivery man that day.

We arrived at the hospital in time and everything seemed to be in order once the experts appeared on the scene.

I found out later that all my fear, pain and anguish that had come over the radio waves were a big hit with all those in the dispatch room that day.

*****

It was late at night and there were two of us working the Seward Highway south of Anchorage. The other patrol unit was Tony, a friend of mine who had gone through the academy with me. We were both rookies.

I heard Tony on the radio making a traffic stop on a possible drunk driver. I decided to head that direction just to check on him in case of problems. There was definitely a problem. As I pulled up to the two vehicles, there was Tony rolling around on the ground with a beautiful blonde woman. It took me a moment to get my laughter under control and get out to assist. She was a woman, but in no way a lady. Her language would put a truck driver to shame. She was very drunk and very combative. Tony finally got her restrained and into his patrol vehicle. While he took her to the post for a Breathalyzer test, I stayed behind to impound her car.

She had left behind, in her car, a mean German Shepherd. I'm sure he wasn't mean around her, but he made sure I knew that I was not welcome anywhere near the vehicle. I tried to reason with him, but he was too busy bashing his teeth against the side window to listen to reason. The wrecker driver was greeted in the same way. I ended up impounding the car with the dog still in it. He stayed there until his owner was released from jail the next day.

Tony's combative drunk driver pled not guilty. She showed up in court dressed like a dignified lady and quite possibly would have been difficult to prosecute. Fortunately, the prosecution had the videotape of her taken during her Breathalyzer test. It showed her to be a loud, obnoxious, foul-mouthed drunk with a severe vicious streak. She immediately became embarrassed. Her attorney, shocked at what he had just seen, advised her to change her plea to guilty. She did.

*****

We were getting a large number of calls from the public concerning the disappearance of their dogs. Dogs had been coming up missing, sometimes from their own yards or on chains. The dogs all seemed to have one thing in common; they were all of the Alaskan sled dog variety.

An occasional caller reported seeing a vehicle that appeared to be a dogcatcher's van in the area at the time of some of the abductions. Whenever we received those calls, we rushed to the area, but there would be no sign of the van. We surmised that, if the van was involved, the driver probably had a police scanner to alert him when we were dispatched.

The remains of the animals were starting to turn up. They had been skinned out and dumped. It turned out that the dog hides were being sold to gullible tourists as wolf hides. One of the buyers had been told by someone that they had been duped and they came to us.

I don't recall if the culprit was ever caught or if he ceased operations because we were getting close to him. I transferred to a different post around that time and didn't hear any more about it.

*****

Back in those days, there were a lot of times when we only had two troopers on a shift. One would take the north side, meaning Muldoon, Eagle River, etc., and the other trooper would take the south side including the Seward Highway. Contrary to what a lot of officials and politicians stated back then, we did have somewhat of an organized crime problem in Anchorage along with all the traffic accidents, domestic disputes, burglaries and assaults going on. Two troopers per shift were about a fifth of what we needed. There were nights I remember when we could respond only to felony calls. Anything else had to wait for the day shift the next day. It was very hectic, fast-paced and fun! Very exciting times!

Still, Anchorage was too big a town for me. I was ready to get out of the headquarters office with all the "big brass" around and get out in a more rural setting. Linda and I heard there was an opening in Delta Junction. We put in our application for the Delta post after working in Anchorage for three months. We got the transfer and put our house up for sale. We were to join two other troopers who would be stationed there. Delta would turn out to be a very busy post.

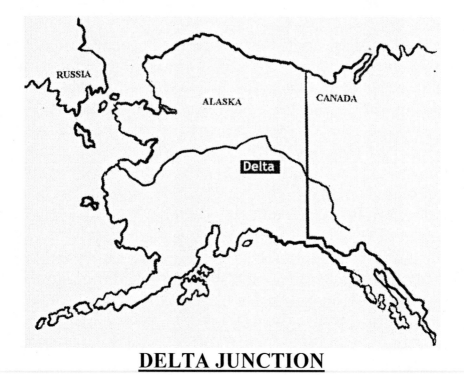

# DELTA JUNCTION

In June of 1974 Linda, Darin, Chad and I were driving into Delta for the first time. It was an exciting move. We had the boys singing "Home on the Range" as we drove the last ten miles into town, because we knew there were bison in the area. We fell in love with the Delta area right away.

Delta is a small town located at the junction of the Alaska and Richardson Highways. The area has a beautiful and varied terrain. You can travel out of Delta in three different directions by road and each road goes through completely different terrain. Following the Richardson Highway northwest would take you through a hundred miles of hilly country to Fairbanks. The Alaska Highway to the southeast leads you through mountains and numerous rivers to Tok (pronounced Toke) and then east to the Alaska/Canada border. The Richardson Highway south will lead you up over a high mountain pass with rugged snow-capped mountains on both sides and glaciers. There was a lifetime of wilderness country filled with wild animals, perfect for a young family with adventurous blood to do their hiking, fishing and exploring.

The town had no side streets, just the highway going through the middle of it. There was a lumberyard, general store, liquor store, bank, trooper post/courthouse, and four bars.

The building of the Alaska Pipeline was just getting under way when we moved to Delta, and there was a pipeline construction camp located just a few miles outside of town.

The previous single trooper had quit and left the town without any form of law enforcement for a few months. The local people had gotten used to that idea and were getting drunk and racing their cars up and down the highway right through the middle of town. The middle of town just happened to be where we three troopers had moved into our state-owned housing. It didn't take long for the locals to learn that we were there and active.

*****

Our mobile home was secured tightly to a cement foundation, because, we later learned, a previous mobile home on that site had been hit by the famous Delta wind and had been sent across the field rolled up into a ball. All three of our homes contained police radios. Our wives would be our dispatchers. We had one business phone number with an extension phone in each home and one at the post. It was like a party line. You only answered the phone if you were on duty. We also had an intercom system between the three homes and the post. Each of our homes also contained a bank alarm, which would warn us of any problem at the local bank, which was located on the edge of town.

We had been advised before leaving Anchorage that our state housing in Delta was completely furnished, so we sold all of our furniture, beds and all, prior to making the move. Poor Linda! I felt sorry for her when we walked into the trailer to find it empty except for a telephone sitting on the floor.

We called the Fairbanks headquarters and the Lieutenant came down to Delta the next day to look over the situation. He was great with us and inspired us with confidence that something would be done right away. Within a few days, a truck full of new furnishings arrived and we were finally able to get settled in our new home.

Later that winter when the temperatures dropped, we found that the mobile home had not been built with Alaska winters in mind. The oil furnace ran continuously, which was dangerous, and still, the bottom two feet of the living room drapes were frozen to the walls with ice about an inch thick. The boys' blankets on their beds would freeze to the walls overnight. We could have used the space between the back of the couch and the wall for refrigeration if we had needed it. Every window was completely frosted over except for one little baseball-sized spot on one front window. That's where we would peek out to watch for the school bus. We couldn't let the boys venture out to the bus stop until the bus actually arrived, as it was too cold at times for them to stand out there. Then they waddled out in all their snow gear looking like two robots.

We really didn't mind the inconveniences of the extreme cold. We found the experience humorous at times and joked about it. We were young, excited, having fun and enjoying our new adventure.

Out in the side yard of our residence was an old weather-beaten shed. It was about four feet wide and eight feet long. There were no windows—just a solid wooden door. It was in sad shape. It had been the local jail before the new one was built across the highway from us.

The new trooper post contained two desks, a microfiche for checking on driver's licenses and vehicle license plates, law books and two jail cells. Oh, and, of course, a coffee pot. The other half of the one-story building held the courtroom presided over by Magistrate Hershel Crutchfield. He was very supportive of the troopers and took his job seriously. He was good at his job and was, in later years, promoted and sent to Fairbanks.

*****

We had a wide variety of people in Delta, which led to numerous problems. There were the locals who made their living in areas such as farming, retail sales, government work, or working for the newly arrived pipeline camp. There were also the non-resident pipeliners who were mostly from Texas. We had soldiers from the local army base at Fort Greely, numerous hitchhiking transients and the Sleepy Hollow bunch. Yes, we had Sleepy Hollow people. They were a strange bunch who lived back in the bush off a dirt trail and were trying to remain old fashioned in a relatively modern world. They had a hand painted sign on their trail that read, "If you enter Sleepy Hollow, be prepared to step back 50 years or you won't come out alive."

Linda and I worked together giving driver's tests and issuing driver's licenses. (Another trooper wife's "volunteer" job) When we three troopers started cracking down on drivers and their licenses, many of the Sleepy Hollow people hurried in to get their outdated licenses renewed. This is the honest truth—one man's license had not been renewed for so many years that it was handwritten! I only wish I could remember the date on it, but I can't.

The amazing thing about the different groups of people I mentioned previously is that none of them got along. This was never more obvious than in the bars. We had one bar in particular, the most popular bar in town, where many fights took place. After repeatedly receiving calls to come and break up bar-fights, we troopers recommended to the owner that he hire someone who might be able to keep the peace and stop the fights before they got out of control. He knew just the guy! The guy he hired turned out to be a bigger problem as he was tougher than any three guys combined in town, and he loved to fight. The bar-fight calls to us came to a stop all right, but we got word of too many patrons getting roughed up. So we then had to recommend to the bar owner to either calm down his new employee or get rid of him.

We had an old town drunk who would get smashed at the bars and then walk around some nights unable to find where he had parked his car. It was always parked right in front of the bar. He would walk over to our trailer across the highway from the bar and report his car stolen. We would find his car for him and get him a ride home or take him home ourselves. One night he insisted on driving his vehicle home. I couldn't convince him otherwise, so when he started the engine, I placed him under arrest for operating a motor vehicle while intoxicated (OMVI back then), and transported him the 500 yards or so to the jail. He was an old gaffer with a bad heart. He was getting himself all worked up into a frenzy and I began to worry that he might have a heart attack. I contacted the local physician's assistant and then the magistrate. We decided we had better get him out of the jail cell and take him home as he was getting hysterical. Well, that seemed to work out okay.

The next morning he came knocking on our door to report that his car had been stolen again. It was still parked in the bar parking lot where I had arrested him the night before.

That same day I began the necessary paperwork to try to get his driving license revoked. He was 83 years old and legally blind, but still had a valid driver's license. He had a special hunting license for the legally blind where another hunter could hunt for him. He was a serious alcoholic. On top of all that he had a bum leg that he dragged when he walked, because he couldn't lift it. Should have been easy to get his license revoked, shouldn't it? Well, it wasn't. There was no legal way to get it done. I was told we would have to put up with him for another year until his license expired and then refuse to reissue it. We were livid. It was an accident looking for a place to happen. And, it did. One day in broad daylight, while he was drunk, he crossed the centerline hitting another car head on. Fortunately, the family in the other car was uninjured, but the old man's leg injuries prevented him from ever driving again.

*****

A number of comical incidents happened while we were stationed in Delta. One of them was the "Case of the Barefoot Burglar". I received a call one night about a lodge

19

out on the Clearwater River that had been broken into and money stolen from a secret cabinet.

As I approached the lodge, with flashlight in hand, I did a walk-around checking all four sides of the building. I was dumbstruck! (Whatever that really means) There in the two feet of snow in the twenty below zero temperature was a set of footprints. Not boot prints, but *bare footprints.* They went up to a window, which had been broken from the outside. The burglar then had walked across the barroom, located the money and went back out the same window. The tracks then went a few hundred yards to where he had parked his vehicle.

I took photos and drew sketches of the footprints and tire tracks. I interviewed the few people who were in the living quarters portion of the lodge, took foot measurements and eliminated them as suspects. It was pretty apparent that whoever the barefoot burglar was, he was going to be suffering some foot damage.

I put out the word around town and it wasn't long before the bar directly across the street from us called and said a kid showed up there with frostbitten feet. I picked him up. He was 17 years old. He was very forthcoming and talkative. He said he knew we could identify boot prints and figured if he went barefoot, we wouldn't be able to track him down.

*****

Then there was the case of the "Peanut Picker". This story is somewhat of an embarrassment to me, but I'll include it anyway. While driving through town late one night, I saw a tractor-trailer rig parked near the highway in the parking lot of one of the local bars. The side door on the trailer was open and I saw movement in the dark interior. Thinking that possibly someone was getting into the contents while the driver was in the bar eating, I turned my patrol car around and came up along side the trailer door with my window down. I shined my spotlight inside the door and instantly saw a large gray object come reaching out of the trailer toward my face. Whatever the object was, it had a finger-like protuberance on the end of it. It happened so fast that, even though I was seat-belted in, I felt the car roof crushing the top of my Stetson as I nearly jumped out of my skin. Then I realized that there was an elephant in there. He had thrust his trunk toward me when I shined the light inside the trailer.

As I got out of the patrol car and walked around to the driver's side of the rig, I saw "Jumbo the Elephant" painted on the trailer in large letters. I checked the cab and found the driver sleeping. After I had awakened him, he said that whenever he stopped the rig, he had to open the trailer door for Jumbo, or he would get nervous and start rocking the trailer. I made the mistake of letting my friends know about the "Jumbo" incident and took serious ribbing for a long time afterward.

\*\*\*\*\*

Alaskans love to pick on Texans more than anybody. But, let's face it; they just ask for it. In 1974 there were a lot of trucks coming through Delta. Some of them came from Anchorage, while some came from the "Lower Forty-eight" states. A lot of them came from Texas and Oklahoma hauling pipeline supplies up through Canada by way of the Alaska Highway. Once they crossed the Canada/Alaska border, they drove through Tok, Delta and on north to

Prudhoe Bay on the coast of the Arctic Ocean. Some of them were hauling extra long sections of four-foot diameter pipe for the pipeline on specially designed trailers. These rigs were over a hundred feet long.

Most of the drivers were very competent. Then there were the Texans. They were the ones who were unable to walk around their trucks without slipping and falling time after time on the snow and ice because of their pointy-toed, slick-soled cowboy boots. They cursed the cold while wearing a light jean jacket and cowboy hat while a parka and fur hat would have been much more appropriate. It was obvious that they were not used to driving in the snow. I remember helping Texans chain up their tires on several occasions at the bottom of Shaw Creek hill north of Delta. While we were chaining up, many local truck drivers would go by honking their horns and then steadily climb the long, steep grade of Shaw Creek hill without chains! It really does make a big difference when a driver is used to slippery road conditions. Even though we all realized that, the Texas drivers who couldn't walk or drive in the snow were the butt of many jokes in the restaurants and on the CB's.

*****

The pipeline camp in Delta had an immense economic effect on the little town. The restaurant and bar owners were getting rich, but the average person was adversely affected. The price of rent jumped, as well as the cost of goods and services. A few of the locals could not afford to live in the area any longer and actually had to move away.

The camp itself was very large and very modern. The waste that went on there sickened me. While I believe that the workers deserved the best quality of food available, I couldn't believe what was going on there. Every meal was a banquet with a variety of meats and a large variety of everything else. Long tables covered with food filled the mess hall. No matter how many types of meat were prepared, steak was required to be served at every meal. There was always one long table covered with desserts. The camp cooks were not allowed to serve the workers any broken cookies. They had to be whole. All the chipped or broken cookies were thrown into the dumpsters after each meal along with the tremendous amount of leftovers. There were a lot of families in the area who could have made good use of the food that the camp wasted.

There was another problem with the pipeline camp that made me grind my teeth. They had reported that several portable generators were missing. I went out to investigate and met with the camp manager. It turned out that, yes, there had been some generators stolen.

Further investigation revealed that the camp and the camp manager didn't really care if items were stolen and did nothing to discourage theft. While there was a guard shack and a guard at the gate entrance, they were given no authority to check outgoing vehicles. They could look in the vehicle as it went by, but were not allowed to search it or even to look under tarps in the back of the pickups. It was an easy matter to throw items in the back of a pickup, throw a tarp over it and drive through the gate. It had been happening regularly. These previous incidents just hadn't been reported.

The manager said that his policy was this: Any time they ordered something that they thought the local employees would want at home and would steal, they would order enough for each local employee plus whatever amount the camp would need. Incredible! It was just another example of the waste that went on at that camp.

The manager said that the reason that he reported the latest theft when he had not reported the previous ones, was because he felt that several generators had been taken by one person. The manager figured that the thief would be trying to sell the generators, and that made him mad.

The camp was equipped with many yellow pickups with "Bechtel" painted on the doors. There were Bechtel pickups all over town and all over the countryside. In the winter, each bar would have six or eight yellow pickups parked out in front with the engines running. A bar patron who may or may not have driven there in a yellow pickup, would come out of the bar, hop into a running truck and drive it down to the next bar. There were a number of yellow trucks reported stolen that were later found down the road at one of the other bars. However, there were a lot of those trucks that were actually stolen; not just from the Delta camp, but also from numerous camps along the pipeline. I would venture to say there were dozens stolen. The pipeline people didn't really care. They could always get more. Just from generalized stories I have heard over the years, I know a lot of Bechtel trucks were modified in some ways, repainted and used on Alaskan homesteads for years. It would be interesting to know how many are actually still out there.

During the year I worked in Delta as a "blue shirt", I worked closely with the "brown shirt". (Remember earlier, I said that a "brown shirt" is a trooper who concentrates on the fish and game laws of Alaska.) Jeff Dailey was a good guy and a good Wildlife Officer. He was very effective at his job. On one occasion, a grizzly bear den was located directly in the path of the oil pipeline, which was being constructed. The pipeline folks who had found the den didn't know for a while how lucky they were to still be alive. They had heard that bears hibernate in the winter and do not wake up until spring. Well, that may be true of ground squirrels and marmots, but I can guarantee you that bears are easily aroused and are occasionally out and about in the winter. If those people had known that, they probably would not have been twisting that forked stick into the bear's fur to get some souvenir hairs. They were lucky the bear did not wake up.

When Jeff Dailey saw the situation, he told the pipeline personnel that they would have to discontinue the pipeline where they were and continue it again one quarter mile on the other side of the den. Of course, they were incensed and felt that the bear should be destroyed. After all, the pipeline was a multi-million dollar project. They were eventually forced, against their will, to leave a gap in the pipeline and come back to fill it in the following spring after the bear came out of hibernation.

Linda and I went out to the pipeline camp's open house the next spring and while on a tour of the camp we were shown a large photo of the gap in the pipeline at the bear den. Our host gave a big speech to our group of approximately fifteen people about how interested the pipeliners were in protecting the environment. They had found a bear den on the pipeline route and in the best interest of the bear, had decided to go around it and not disturb him.

Linda and I looked at each other and grinned, because we knew the truth. They would have blown that bear away in a minute if they could have gotten away with it.

*****

25

Winters in Delta are severe. It can get just as cold in Delta as in Fairbanks; however, while Fairbanks doesn't get much wind in the winter, Delta does.

When the temperatures were colder than forty degrees below zero in Delta, school was called off. We saw our thermometer go down to eighty below zero! The three trooper patrol cars had to stay outside as none of us had a garage. In the coldest part of the winter, that caused several problems. We would back the vehicles into our driveways when we arrived home because when the vehicles got extremely cold, we couldn't shift the gears in and out of reverse.

There were three heaters on my rig; one for the dipstick, one on the engine block and one in the vehicle cab. There were still no guarantees that it would start, so I had to leave it running all night when I was on call. Around three o'clock in the morning I would get up and drive over to the Highway Department's garage where I refueled the rig. I would then bring it back home and go to bed leaving the car running. Even when we did everything right and were able to get our vehicles into gear, we still had the problem of all four tires being square on the bottom and frozen that way. Many times we had to drive to emergency situations with "square tires" for several miles until they finally rounded out.

A lot of people make the mistake of driving in the wintertime with their car heater on high and their coat on the back seat. That works fine until you crash your vehicle and are pinned in it, unable to reach your warm gear and get it on. When that happens in severe cold, unless someone arrives on the scene immediately, you are in danger of freezing to death. We never had anyone freeze to death while I was in Delta, but we did send a few accident victims to the hospital with frostbite injuries. Leaving the heater turned down and being dressed warmly could have prevented those injuries.

One of the more interesting accidents I responded to was one that involved a panel van from California with three hippies (I realize that is an old term—I guess I am showing my age) in it. They were coming toward Delta on the Alaska Highway when they collided with a herd of bison crossing the road. They must have been traveling very fast. They killed three bison, which is unusual and remarkable in itself. The van was totally destroyed and was nothing but twisted metal. None of the three occupants were injured, and all they could think of was whether or not I would let them keep the bison meat.

*****

We had many interesting incidents involving bison. They are a beautiful animal and we enjoyed having them around. I remember one moonlit night we were awakened by a couple of sharp barks from our Labrador who was in his doghouse outside. After those two barks, he was silent. I jumped up out of bed and looked out the bedroom window. I was stunned at what I saw. Right under our window about three feet away from the house was an entire herd of bison running by as if they had been stampeded. Even more incredibly, there was no sound. We had about two feet of snow on the ground but still, you would think there would be some kind of rumbling sound. There wasn't. It was dead silent and very eerie with the moon in the background reflecting on the snow and the herd of bison running by.

I told Linda to get up and look. She did and they were still going by. It was like a "ghost" bison herd. It was an exciting experience for both of us. The bison were running within a few feet of our dog's house, and he was cowering in the back of it, not making a peep. That was probably the smartest thing that dog ever did.

I learned two things about bison while living in Delta. They are hard on farmers' crops and they hate snow machines.

If you get too close to a herd while on a snow machine, they will come after you. I suspect that they don't like the noise that the machines make. I have often thought that if I were to drive by a herd and get them to chase me, then jump off the machine and go one way while the machine went the other, they would probably ignore me and go after the machine. It would be an interesting experiment. Fortunately, whenever driving a snow machine, I was always sober enough never to consider it seriously.

*****

We had plenty of moose in the area also. It's not uncommon in Alaska for a moose to fall through thin lake ice. Sometimes they are able to get themselves out and sometimes not.

One day I was flagged down by a local man who said there was a moose trapped in the ice on Quartz Lake just a couple of miles away. We drove back and found her still there about thirty feet off shore. I was able to walk out within ten feet of her and throw a loop from my emergency towrope around her neck. We hooked the other end of the rope onto the back of his four wheel drive pickup, and by pulling very slowly and carefully, the moose was able to get back up on the ice. After about ten minutes of standing and catching her breath, she trotted off into the woods. We had to let her take the rope with her, because there was no way I could get it off from around her neck. I had made a large loop and twisted the rope several times before hooking it to the pickup. That ensured that the moose would be able to slip it off eventually.

That was the first time I had rescued a moose from a lake, but it would not be the last. The second time would come years later in Palmer, Alaska.

*****

I responded to one accident that occurred under strange circumstances, to say the least. A pipeline worker in Fairbanks had begun to hallucinate and behave weirdly. His wife was concerned about his well-being and had come up from the Lower Forty-eight to "rescue" him. They had left Fairbanks and were heading toward Delta in a pickup with a canopy on the back. The canopy was full of his possessions. While en route south, he began talking about how the Devil was after him. His mental state continued to deteriorate until he was accusing his wife in the seat next to him of being the Devil. All the while he was driving faster and faster. Just prior to reaching the Richardson Roadhouse, while trying to push his wife out through the truck door, he lost control of the vehicle. The vehicle left the road and went into the woods. The pickup landed hard and the canopy literally exploded scattering his possessions all over the area. The crazed man took off on foot screaming and running through the woods. His wife walked to the roadhouse to call for help. Neither of them were seriously injured. The man was eventually coaxed out of the woods and taken in for treatment.

While assisting the wrecker driver in removing the vehicle, I noticed a pair of men's briefs hanging high up in a spruce tree. I was hoping that wasn't the pair he was wearing at the time of the accident.

*****

A friend of mine, with whom I went through the academy, was stationed in Copper Center as the Fish and Wildlife Officer. He had flown to Fairbanks in the Department super cub and had stopped by our place to overnight with us on his return home.

Ken spent the evening visiting with us and our two boys. He made a big impression on the boys and they were sorry to see him leave the following morning. Linda offered to make him some sandwiches to take along, but he didn't think he would need them. I drove him to his airplane on the edge of town. He was to check in with Tok along his route home.

Ken didn't call us to let us know that he had made it home safely and we knew that the weather between Delta and Tok was questionable. When we checked with Tok, they had not heard from him. After verifying that he had not made it home to Copper Center, we notified Fairbanks that Ken was missing. We gave them all the information we had and a search was initiated.

Darin and Chad were very upset. They had made a new friend and now he was in trouble. It was winter and temperatures were low. We knew that, wherever he went down, he would be all right unless he was injured. An injured person does not have the ability to withstand severe weather conditions, as does a healthy person. We knew he would have survival gear with him; it was Department policy, as well as required by state law.

To the relief of our entire family and many others, Ken was soon located. He had been forced to land due to weather and was walking out to the highway carrying his ELT (Emergency Locator Transmitter). This was just another of many temporary scares which Alaskans endure when a friend or family member is overdue on a flight. I imagine that Ken had probably wished later that he had accepted those sandwiches Linda had offered.

*****

As I have mentioned earlier, the winter weather in Delta could be cruelly cold. When it gets sixty or seventy degrees below zero, things come to a standstill.

After a stretch of fifty below temperatures, it warmed up to thirty-five below zero. Linda and her good friend, Bea, who happened to the Wildlife Officer's wife, decided that they had better make a trip the hundred miles north to Fairbanks to stock up on groceries before it turned cold again. It was thirty-five below when they left Delta. During the two-hour drive to Fairbanks, the temperature started dropping. They had to leave the car running while they were in the stores for fear it wouldn't start again for them.

By the time they had finished shopping, the car was loaded with groceries and the temperature was down to fifty-five below zero. The car began overheating and the radiator boiled over. They decided to spend the night in Fairbanks with a friend.

The next morning it was seventy-four below zero. They decided to head for home and a couple of troopers told them to stop at several roadhouses along the way back to Delta and call in to let them know they were still okay. Things went as planned until they reached the infamous Shaw Creek hill with it's steep winding curves. (It's one of those hills where you need to come down with one foot out the door and on the pavement to help slow you down.)

The trip down the hill immediately got very exciting for them as they discovered that they had no brakes. The brakes had frozen up. Fortunately, no vehicles were coming up the hill as their car was quickly gaining speed. After a hair-raising ride down the hill, they shot out onto straight level road at the bottom and swore they would not be making any more trips to Fairbanks until spring. Fortunately they reached home safely.

The next morning our thermometer read eighty degrees below zero!

\*\*\*\*\*

One of the other troopers, who happened to be the O.I.C. (officer in charge) and I were riding our snow machines and working on them in front of our house, when Linda stuck her head out the door and said, "The bank alarm is going off!" John and I strapped on our gun belts over our snow machine suits and jumped into our patrol cars. After grabbing our shotguns and exiting our vehicles at the bank, we went through the bank doors; he went through the front door and I went through the side door. Everyone inside the bank was calmly doing their job.

It was a false alarm. Someone had accidentally bumped the alarm button. Everything turned out all right, but we talked afterward about what they must have thought seeing two guys in snow machine suits with stocking caps on their heads coming through the doors with shotguns.

One of the big benefits of working in Alaska and especially in the northern portions of Alaska is that you get to see the northern lights better than just about anywhere in the world. Outside of Delta with no artificial lights to interfere, they are spectacular. The lights were directly overhead, rolling across the sky in great sheets of white, red, blue, green and yellow. They were far better than any fireworks display.

On several nights when the northern lights were especially brilliant, I would radio Linda who was dispatching for me. She would be sleeping on the couch next to the radio with her ears tuned in for my call. I would tell her on the radio to step outside and check the lights. Now to Fairbanks headquarters, that sounded like an official business transmission. Actually it was our code for Linda to go outside and see how beautiful the northern lights were that night.

Wrapped in her blanket, she would shuffle out in the cold and take a look. Since there was a mercury vapor light right outside our door, she didn't get the full effect of the northern lights. I am sure that as she shuffled back into the house she was muttering something about people who wake her up in the middle of the night. I, being so excited and enthused about the aurora borealis, kept sending her back out on occasion to stare up at the mercury vapor light and she, not wanting to hurt my feelings, continued to do so.

October 26, 1974, was Linda's and my twelfth wedding anniversary. Bob Cramer, who was the owner of the local Evergreen Bar and who was an all-around good guy, invited us over to celebrate. He served us our anniversary dinner complete with champagne.

We wanted to dance, but it was too hot to dance with my jacket on. I couldn't dance with it off, because I was wearing my "off-duty" revolver in a holster on my belt. Bob was good enough to sit at our table and hold my jacket and revolver while we danced.

Upon leaving the Evergreen that night, we walked over to the trooper post next door and gave each other a Breathalyzer exam. After drinking two small bottles of champagne, we just barely registered on the scale. We would have had to drink a wheelbarrow full of that stuff to register legally drunk.

*****

Oh, I've got to tell you about the "Ghost of Gerstle River". It's a true story as all the others are.

Late one summer night while patrolling southbound on the Alaska Highway, I was approaching the steel bridge crossing at Gerstle River. I saw, ahead of me, a pair of taillights entering the bridge at a high rate of speed. I speeded up to a rate that I knew would allow me to overtake him. I saw the taillights go across the bridge and then disappear. The road on the other side of the bridge was straight for some distance and there was no apparent way he could have eluded me. I was right on his tail and then he was gone. It was pitch dark out and he could not have turned off his lights and remained on the road. I went home later that night still puzzled.

Several days later in Fairbanks, I mentioned to some of the troops that I had seen a weird sight at Gerstle River the other night. One of them said, "Oh, you saw the Ghost of Gerstle River, huh?" He then proceeded to tell me that other troopers previously stationed in Delta had claimed to see taillights going across the bridge and then disappear. He figured it was some type of reflection from my headlights. I don't think so. I'm still not sure what it was.

*****

There was a trapper living with his family between Dot Lake and Delta on the Alaska Highway. He was trapping lynx and there was an abundance of them in the area. He hadn't been able to get a moose for his winter meat his first year there, so they lived on rabbits. Chief Issac, the Athabascan chief of the Dot Lake Tribe, asked the trapper what he was doing with his lynx carcasses. He had been skinning them and discarding the meat. Chief Isaac told him that lynx meat was very good to eat and was nutritious. He was right. One day while I was visiting, the trapper sliced some steaks off the hindquarters of a lynx, butterflied them and fried them. They were very tasty and reminded me of pork chops.

*****

The most interesting wedding I have ever attended took place at Dot Lake. One of our Troopers from Tok had met a girl from back East on the Alaska Highway. Carl and Margie decided to get married. Chief Isaac of Dot Lake offered to give them a traditional Indian wedding ceremony.

Last day as a "blue shirt" before transferring to Kodiak as a "brown shirt." (Photo by Linda Carpenter)

The ceremony was beautiful with tribal members in traditional beaded dress and the wedding was marked with symbolism. Carl and Margie were each given valuable Hudson Bay blankets. They stood on a white one during the ceremony.

There was lots of food and dancing to the drums and chanting. Even our oldest son, Darin, who was ten years old at the time, got caught up in the excitement and was dancing to the drums along with the Dot Lake Tribe. Carl was honored with an Indian name and then the ceremony was over. In all, it must have taken about two or three hours to complete the wedding.

From Dot Lake, we all traveled to Tok where Carl and Margie were married again by a justice of the peace in a very fast and dull ceremony. Carl then put Margie on a dogsled (her first ride) and mushed the team over to the Tok Lodge where the reception was held. Carl had worked the night before preparing a big feast, which included nearly every type of wild game available in Alaska. The food was great.

Toward the end of the evening, a couple of on-duty troopers came in, pronounced Carl drunk and hauled him away to jail. Margie had to go around to the guests to try to collect donations for "bail" money so she could get Carl out of jail. They traveled by snow machine to a remote cabin where they spent their honeymoon, but we weren't invited to that portion of the ritual.

*****

One of my scarier moments in Delta was one night when I received a call to respond to a domestic dispute. Upon arriving at the trailer home, I heard screaming coming from inside. I went through the door and found a terrified woman looking in my direction. Off to my right, in the center of the kitchen, was her husband holding their baby up to his chest with a kitchen knife at the baby's throat. He was mad at his wife and told her he was going to kill the baby. He was deadly serious.

Over the next twenty minutes I stood holding my service revolver aimed at his head, while about ten feet away, he stood, still holding the knife at the baby's throat. His wife was off to one side screaming at him, and I was talking a mile a minute trying to calm him down.

Finally, he lowered the knife and dropped it. I told the wife to take the baby. As soon as she did, I grabbed the husband and arrested him. It had been a very tense stand off and I think we were all relieved when it was over.

*****

After awhile, I started to realize that while I was breaking up bar fights and chasing taillights, the Wildlife Trooper was doing the things for which I had actually come to Alaska. He was running the riverboat and climbing sheep mountains as part of his duty. In 1975, Linda and I put in for a transfer to the "brown shirts" (Wildlife Protection). We were accepted and offered a choice of transferring to either Valdez or Kodiak Island. Luckily, we picked Kodiak, which was a great place for a family. It turned out to be one of our most enjoyable posts.

*****

# KODIAK ISLAND TOUR

We left Delta in high spirits and anticipating an exciting duty post in Kodiak. The four of us and our black Lab dog traveled in our 1972 Chevy Blazer pulling a thirteen-foot camper trailer. We were looking forward to living near the salt water.

We traveled approximately 600 miles to Homer where we drove our rig onto the state ferry "Trusty Tusty" (Tustemena) and sailed southward to Kodiak Island.

The voyage was not at all pleasant. It was an all day trip from morning until late night. The weather was fierce. We had high winds creating high seas. We passed the Barren Islands along the way. The Barren Islands were known for being in a severe weather area and they lived up to their reputation that night.

The Tustemena was very seaworthy, but it was still unsettling the way it was being tossed about by the angry waves. The seating area contained movie theater-type seats with armrests. All passengers were seated and holding on tight to avoid being ejected. We watched as the wall of water on one side of the ship raised higher and higher. It would then drop as the water on the other side raised higher and higher. One of the heavy metal outside doors behind us came open and started swinging. It banged upon opening as it hit the wall, and then banged as it swung back. This went on for several minutes until I had had enough and decided to get up and close it.

Linda says she still remembers, with some amusement, the scene which took place. My attempts to walk toward the door were very similar to what I would imagine it would be like to try walking up a slide in an upright position without holding on. And, then having someone rock the slide! With much effort, I would work my way uphill toward the door as the ship rocked. Then suddenly I would be back peddling to avoid picking up speed enough to crash through the wall behind me. Back and forth with each roll of the ship, sometimes I would be in an uncontrolled jog in forward gear and sometimes in reverse gear.

Finally, I was able to reach the door and get it closed and secured. Then began the arduous journey back to my seat.

*****

Kodiak, the emerald isle…. I have heard it called the northernmost island of the Hawaiian Chain, however, it grows the least pineapples.

When we arrived there to begin our new duty assignment in June 1975, it was raining. It continued to rain for most of the two years we were there. Kodiak was still quite possibly our favorite post while with the Department.

40

It was an ideal place to raise two boys, ages eight and ten. The boys could walk down to the bay and fish for salmon from the beach. We had a boat and some crab pots. We only had to run our boat for ten minutes out of the harbor to a nearby island where we could fill a couple of buckets with clams and catch salmon from the beach. We would then pick our crab pots on the way back to the boat harbor. Our crab pots always produced big king crabs. Life was good!

Kodiak even had a grunion run (small sardine-like fish) down by Chiniak Point, which was fun. The females ride the surf up onto the beach where they lay their eggs, then they would ride the next wave back out to sea. The following wave would bring in the males who fertilized the eggs and would then ride the next wave out. This was a continuous cycle, which always left a line of shimmering fish at the waterline to be picked up by hand and thrown into a bucket.

We had a different system set up for collecting the grunion. We camped on top of a steep thirty or forty-foot hill. We kept the bucket up there and had the kids pack the fish, one or two at a time up the hill to the bucket. By using this method, the kids were entertained for a much longer period of time and we didn't get too many fish. It never seemed to occur to the kids that it would be much easier to take the bucket down to the water's edge. We adults sat around a nice campfire visiting while the kids did all the work.

*****

Kodiak is an island sixty miles wide and one hundred miles long with numerous bays, each several miles deep which amounted to a very large area for the five or six

Wildlife Officers assigned there. In addition, Afognak Island and Raspberry Island were in our patrol area. Even many Alaskans do not realize that there are elk in Alaska. Both Afognak and Raspberry Islands are home to a sizable group of transplanted Roosevelt elk. Because of the local feed, they tend to have larger bodies and smaller antlers than their southern relatives.

There is also a wild reindeer herd on the island, which is not very well known. In the early 1900's the U.S. government transplanted domestic reindeer there for the natives to herd. The problem, of course, was that the Kodiak natives were not herders and eventually the reindeer became wild. When I was stationed in Kodiak, there was no closed hunting season on the wild reindeer and no limit. I don't know what today's regulations allow.

The Kodiak post was equipped with a twenty-five foot Bertram boat, a twenty-one foot Boston Whaler and a seventeen-foot Boston Whaler. We also had a sixty-foot patrol boat (the PV Trooper) on which several additional officers (marine Wildlife Officers) were assigned. The PV Trooper was out on the open sea more than it was around the close in areas like those of us who were assigned to the Kodiak post.

The terrain on Kodiak varies as the east side is higher in elevation and supports Sitka spruce and cottonwood trees. There are also some alder trees. I know that, because we used mainly alder for firewood. Most of the alder, along with the muskeg, was on the west side of the island. The one thing that the entire island has in common from one place to the next is a lot of Kodiak brown bears. Lots of 1,500 pound brown bears!

The bears eat quite well. Their wide variety of meals includes wild game, blueberries, cranberries, salmon (20 to

40 a day), wild parsnips, grubs, beetles and dead sea animals that have washed ashore.

I never traveled that part of the country without a good strong five cell electric torch and a rifle of at least 30-06 caliber or a pump action shotgun. My main goal was to avoid seeing the inside of a bear.

*****

My introduction to salt water navigation was a quick one. I had spent very little time on the salt water and did not have any navigation experience. When I arrived on the job, sometime during my first week there, my sergeant threw me the keys to a Boston Whaler and said, "This is your island, go to work."

There were charts for us to use, and as I learned over the next two years, there is a lot of important information on those charts. A short chart reading class would have been nice. I had noticed a bunch of asterisks around the island close to the shoreline on the chart, but I never observed anything out there on the water in those areas. After about a week or two of running in and out of the bays, I finally figured out that those asterisks represented hazardous rocks which were sometimes hidden just below the surface of the water!

From personal experiences, I was learning more and more about the tides. Sometimes it could come in and strand you from your boat for several hours and sometimes it would go out, leaving you high and dry. I was lucky. I survived with no major mishaps.

Author's sons, Darin and Chad, after harvesting
king crab and butter clams (Photo by author)

Those of us stationed at the Kodiak post could go home to our families at night, while the marine Wildlife Officers would leave the harbor on the "Trooper" and be gone for two to six weeks at a time. They were usually short one crewman and those of us assigned to the post would take turns going out with them. Nearly every trip out involved fun, excitement, adventure and danger. When working on the "Trooper" we stopped and checked boats and fishermen on board. We chased boats, rode out high seas, traveled long distances, fought fires with our on-board water gun, and sometimes limped home with the "Trooper" covered with ice, which could become extreme enough to roll the boat over and sink it. But, we had fun too, as the following incident suggests.

It was late at night and the seas were high. The waves were rolling us one way and then the other. We were running dark, meaning no lights, interior or exterior. There were several fishing boats in the area and we wanted to make it to a particular location without the fishermen spotting and identifying us as they normally could with our particular light configuration. So there we were, five of us, all standing up in the wheelhouse in the dark. With the rock and roll of the boat in the dark, we were all starting to feel a little queasy. When you start feeling seasick, eating saltine crackers seems to help. I left the wheelhouse and went down to the galley, feeling my way in the dark. Upon reaching the galley, I located the saltines on top of the

45

refrigerator where we kept them. I opened the box, removed one of the cellophane packages and continued, in the dark, back up to the totally dark wheelhouse. We passed the package of crackers around and ate them until they were gone. They weren't very fresh...in fact they seemed to be a little soggy. But, what the heck! They would still do the job.

A couple of the guys wanted me to go back for another package. I again took the box from the top of the refrigerator and removed a package. This time I opened the package and cracked open the refrigerator door to check out the crackers by the light inside. My God! The crackers were all thoroughly covered with a green mold! Yuck!

Of course, being the thoughtful and considerate type of person that I am, I wanted to make sure the rest of the crew shared in the news and immediately returned to the wheelhouse to show everyone what we had been eating. Now, saltines are supposed to quell the nausea that leads to vomiting, but if I remember right, those crackers that night seemed to have the exact opposite effect as everyone immediately scattered in different directions.

*****

Kodiak was a very interesting place to live. The population was made up of a wide variety of cultures including Russian, Norwegian, Swede, Aleut, Filipino and probably several others.

*****

Solly's Tavern had a well-known reputation. It had been written up in a national news magazine as the roughest bar in the nation. A bar full of commercial fishermen can cause a lot of damage in a short period of time. Fortunately, it was within the city limits and was in the jurisdiction of the Kodiak Police Department, not ours.

A very attractive friend of ours was the first female officer hired by the Kodiak Police Department. While the male officers would go in to bar-fights and occasionally get involved in them themselves, Karen could go in and calm everyone down. Nobody wanted to hit her.

Karen later went to work for the Anchorage Police Department and has done exceptionally well for herself. She is very skilled and highly thought of by her peers. She easily dispels the myth that women do not make as good a law officer as men.

The Kodiak bars had their good times too. Like the day two fishermen came in, one with a plastic bag of cooked oatmeal in his coat pocket. When the barkeep wasn't looking, he dumped it on the bar in from of him. His partner, who was in on the joke, started cussing him out for "throwing up" on the Bar. When the barkeep tried to clean up the mess, the second man wouldn't let him. Then, to the chagrin of everyone in the place, he gave his buddy a spoon and made him eat it on the spot. That little practical joke was such a hit with the bar patrons that we heard about it many times over during our two years in Kodiak.

*****

Pillar Mountain is on the very edge of the town of Kodiak. It's actually a very large hill and was the sanctuary many of the local people sought to escape the tsunami (tidal wave) after the 1964 Alaska earthquake. Many people were killed in Kodiak, not by the earthquake, but by the resulting tsunami. There has been a number assigned as to how many deaths resulted in Kodiak, but the locals say that number is not accurate. They feel many more people were killed than the number reflects. They will tell you that before the earthquake, there were a large number of winos and street people laying around the town and boat harbor. They believe the tsunami washed many of them out to sea. A lot of those people had no one to report them missing and were never counted.

*****

One time we were patrolling the commercial fishery in the Grumman Goose. That is a vintage aircraft that is amphibious and, because of its size and weight, is ideal for the fierce weather seen in the Kodiak area.

We were working the northwest area of the island. Several large fishing vessels had gone up into the shallow water at the mouth of a river, which was teeming with salmon. This area was closed to fishing because the salmon were trying to spawn. The fishermen had laid out their nets and were expecting to make a big haul. However, they found themselves in trouble when the tide went out, leaving their boats sitting on the bottom and their fishing nets out of the water and draped across the rocks.

We were unable to land in the mud so we flew over them several times taking photos and logging the incident in our notebooks. We flew back to Kodiak, started all the legal paperwork and nailed them when they came into town the next day. Their fish were seized, sold to the cannery, and the checks were turned over to the state. It was a good feeling to know that "creek robbers" like that didn't always get away.

\*\*\*\*\*

One day we seized a 100-foot fishing vessel called the "Tara Dawn" for a serious crab fishing violation. It was valued at a million dollars, which at that time was an expensive boat. It was the most expensive boat our department had seized up to that point. Now that we had custody of the boat, we were legally responsible for its safety. Since we had had a skipper previously sneak onto his boat after we had seized it and intentionally sink it to collect insurance money from the state, we decided that we needed to stand guard on the "Tara Dawn".

We took turns doing guard duty. It went on for months, waiting for trial and forfeiture of the boat to the state. We were on the lookout for the possibility of someone diving under the boat and attaching explosives.

One evening I was walking the deck and checking the water in the area. I saw bubbles surfacing as from a diver. I contacted the Coast Guard as we had secured the boat in their harbor and asked if they had any divers in the area. They said, "No." I told them to notify my supervisor what was going on. I grabbed the 870 Remington shotgun from the wheelhouse and relocated the bubbles. As I waited to see who would surface, I was expecting a confrontation.

Luckily, about that time, a Fish & Game vehicle drove up and a biologist exited to pick up the "biologist" who was diving there. Either they had not notified the Coast Guard they would be diving there or the Coast Guard did not record it. That diver was luckier than he knew. He should have known better than to dive around a boat that he knew we had seized.

Author's lovely wife, Linda, on the PV "Trooper" with
the "Tara Dawn" in background (Photo by author)

\*\*\*\*\*

Speaking of crab boats, some very miserable but comical nights were spent on the boats at the cannery when we were checking the size of the crabs on board. We had some aluminum devices that we could hold up to each crab and quickly determine if it was of legal size.

Imagine three or four guys standing in a live holding tank, drained of water, along with thousands of crabs. Now imagine all of them trying to hold on to a crab and measure it while jumping about and blurting out language unfit for even a commercial fisherman to hear. That was usually caused by crabs that had grabbed onto and were hanging off of our fingers and our backsides.

The giant king crab, which could easily break your finger, were docile gentlemen and were never a problem. It was the feisty little Dungeness crabs who were quick and always ready for a fight. Seriously, when you reached for one he would stand up on his hind legs and snap his claws at you. It was always funny when it was one of the other guys getting pinched. Sometimes this would go on until the wee hours of the morning. It must have sounded comical to anyone walking by on the dock.

\*\*\*\*\*

Although it rains most of the winter in Kodiak, it does snow occasionally. During our first winter there, we took the boys to the top of Pillar Mountain where we really enjoyed sliding down the slopes on cardboard and pieces of Visqueen. For Christmas our second winter, we gave the boys sleds. Not a flake of snow fell that year... Just rain, rain and more rain.

Two of the troopers I worked with donated their time dressing up as Santa Claus and visiting the kids of their friends. They went separately, of course. One morning they came to work telling of their experience the previous night.

While making his rounds, Mike, who was wearing his Santa suit, spotted another man dressed as Santa stuck in the snow with his vehicle. As Mike was helping push the car, John, another Santa, came by and also stopped to help push. They said they would never forget the looks on the faces of some kids who looked out their windows and saw three different Santa Claus' trying to get the car unstuck.

*****

John, dressed as Santa, came by our house to visit our two boys on Christmas Eve and he was terrific. His costume was superb. We had given him a gift for each of our boys that they had especially wanted and asked for specifically. He parked down the road and ran up to the house with his jingle bells ringing loud and clear. The boys opened their gifts while "Santa" was there and they were very impressed. That night, they believed!

*****

Salmon was very plentiful and we enjoyed eating it. We eventually began to tire of plain baked salmon however, and Linda had to use her imagination to come up with different ways of serving it.

One way she prepared salmon was to lay two unskinned fillets side by side on a baking pan with the skin side down. On one fillet, she spread a thick layer of mayonnaise topped with salt pepper, paprika and parsley flakes. On the other fillet she spread just barbeque sauce. After baking, the mayonnaise on the one fillet had a fluffy texture. We enjoyed this combination for a while and whenever it was served to guests, it went over quite well.

Another great way to prepare salmon was to squeeze lemon juice on a fillet, salt and pepper, then top it with thin lemon slices and lots of sliced onions. We would then wrap it in foil and place it on the grill. If you like salmon moist, this is the way to do it.

Of course, it is hard to beat inch and a half thick salmon steaks placed directly on the grill.

Two popular ways to prepare salmon that we have always liked are smoked and canned. There is no better gift package than a few cans of Alaskan salmon that have been skinned, filleted and chunked into beautiful pieces of red "meat".

*****

One day during the summer salmon fishery, I had gone out on patrol with the crew of the "Trooper" towing our smaller 17-foot Boston Whaler. As we approached Uganik Bay, I jumped into the Whaler and separated from the larger boat to patrol on my own.

At the mouth of Uganik Bay is a small lagoon which I enjoyed entering occasionally because it is such a beautiful spot. The entrance to the lagoon is difficult to locate and during the lower tides, the entrance corridor is too shallow for the bigger fishing boats to navigate. Once inside, the lagoon is about fifty yards by fifty yards in dimension. The surrounding banks and trees make it a paradise. I made sure that I learned the entrance well because if I ever got caught out in a serious storm with poor visibility, that calm little

53

lagoon would be a haven and could possibly make the difference between surviving and not surviving. I would love to go back some day and anchor up in that lagoon for a week or two.

On this particular occasion I continued on into Uganik Bay and saw a fishing boat in the distance. I heard some loud explosions and was convinced that they were throwing dynamite into the water. As I got closer, however, I saw that the "explosions" were actually a killer whale jumping completely out of the water and causing more of a ruckus with his belly flops than even I do with mine. I was able to get a photograph of him in mid-air and later learned that some photographers spend years trying to get photos like that. I never take nature for granted. I fully appreciate every experience I've been lucky enough to have over the years involving nature and her creatures.

It's a known fact that killer whales are very intelligent animals. Some of the Kodiak fishermen claimed to have seen them jump over a rock pile and knock seals or sea lions off the rocks with their tails. Then they would come around and catch them in the water.

When a sea lion is seriously injured, he will try to climb up out of the water onto the rocks or anything handy. I have never seen it occur, but the fishermen talked of injured sea lions (probably injured by their bullets) trying to get into their skiffs and flipping it over tossing out the occupant. Sea lions are incredibly big. I have seen them up close on many occasions and they look like an ocean-going brown bear.

*****

Linda and I bought a beautiful piece of property down at Mill Bay where we thought we might build a home if we stayed in Kodiak. It was heavily wooded with hundred-foot tall Sitka spruce and the bay was excellent for salmon fishing. There were no neighbors close by.

I had planned to catch rain water (of which we had more than enough) with the roof of the house and divert it by way of the rain gutters into a cistern. There would be no shortage of water. I also considered topping one of the taller spruce trees and installing a windmill on top. (We had no shortage of wind either.) With a bank of storage batteries we would always have electricity. People on Kodiak grow great gardens. With all the available fish and shellfish plus an abundance of deer, we would be almost self-sufficient.

A friend of mine bought an adjoining piece of property. We decided we each needed a septic tank and a leach field.

One day while I was out at the Coast Guard base, I saw a pair of dry dock tanks, attached to each other by bolts and angle iron, floating in the water about ninety percent submerged. I went in and told the Coast Guard about the "navigational hazard". I advised them that I would be willing to come by after I got off duty and haul them away if they would load them on the truck for me.

After work, I rented a large flatbed truck from the Chevron station and drove out to the base. Coast Guard personnel hooked onto the tanks, filled with about three thousand gallons of water (1,500 gal. each), and lifted them out of the water using the boom on the Coast Guard cutter "Storis". Even the "Storis" rolled to one side with the weight. After some of the water had drained, they set the tanks on the back of my rented truck and you could hear it groan and settle. After much more draining, the load became light enough to transport and off I went. I drove through town and on out to Mill Bay continually draining water in several different directions.

When I got the tanks on site, the only way we could get them off the truck was to chain them to a spruce tree and drive out from under them. We took them apart, used a cutting torch to make the required openings and set them in the ground. After digging a leach field and laying the pipe, we had our septic systems. The inspector who came was very impressed with the septic tanks and heartily approved the system.

Immediately afterward, the Borough made the use of anything other than a certified septic tank illegal. So everyone thereafter would have to spend more money for a system.

*****

One winter day Wayne, a fellow Wildlife Officer, and I were headed out on a patrol with the Department's International Scout. We were driving east of town toward Chiniak. We came to a very steep, downhill portion of the road that curved sharply to the right halfway down. Freezing rain had coated the road surface with glare ice and we soon realized that we had no braking traction. As we kept gaining more speed, it became painfully apparent that we would never be able to negotiate the curve ahead. The fear that we at first felt was now gone. It was replaced by sheer terror.

When we reached the right-handed curve we would shoot straight off the cliff and do a less than graceful swan dive for over a hundred feet to the rocks and surf below. I told Wayne to steer into the ditch on the right, which he was able to do. We rolled the Scout, but jumped out of the rig grateful to be alive. The Scout had been assigned to Lieutenant Lockman and he was very proud of it. So we were glad to see that it had suffered little damage. That is, until the wrecker driver arrived, wrapped his cable around it and rolled it over again to bring it back up on the road. Then the top and windows were demolished. Wayne and I weren't looking forward to going back and telling the Lieutenant what happened to his Scout.

*****

Later on, I started having stomach problems and learned that the Scout rollover had broken loose some internal stitches. (From being shot in the stomach in 1958 with a 22-caliber rifle my freshman year in high school). I went to the hospital to get the stitches repaired by the only surgeon we had in town (Let's call him Dr. No). A few weeks later I was out in the Whaler by myself a long way from town when I noticed my stomach felt damp and sticky. My body was rejecting some of the stitches and was spitting them back out.

I hailed a large crab boat heading for town and tied off to their stern. I sat in the galley and drank coffee with some of the crew for the remainder of the day until we reached town.

Being a slow learner, I went back to see "Dr. No". He said that during the surgery he had put in some silk stitches, ran out of silk and used steel for the remaining stitches. Some people are allergic to silk stitches (now he thinks of that). He would have to reach into the tiny stitch holes in my belly with a special instrument to clip the silk stitches, and then reach in with special needle-nose pliers to pull the stitches out.

"Dr. No" had me lay on my back on a steel table while he performed this delicate operation. He then promptly forgot which stitches were silk and which were steel. He would have to probe in each hole until he could tell the silk stitches and clip them. This went pretty well until the time came to pull them out. They came out very hard. Also, he had mistakenly grabbed onto a couple of the steel stitches and was literally lifting me off the table. This wouldn't have been quite so bad except he had decided that a painkiller would not be necessary for such a simple job. As you have probably guessed by now, when I got out of there, I never went back to him.

A month or two later, I learned of a new surgeon who was working in Kodiak for just a few months before leaving for California. I went to see him and he was appalled at the job the previous doctor had done on me. Even the scar from the incision on my stomach was twice as wide as it should have been. Dr. Dunbar redid the entire surgery and did it right.

*****

In a later incident, Wayne was on board the 60-foot "Trooper" towing the 17-foot Whaler along behind. He jumped into the Whaler to leave the bigger boat and started it up. He ran alongside the "Trooper" and turned in front of it to leave the area. Then his outboard motor quit. There he was standing in a small boat with a much larger boat bearing down on him. It turned out that the "Trooper" was on automatic pilot and the crew who had been on the deck with Wayne did not see his predicament. To avoid being run over, Wayne jumped out of the Whaler. It turned out to be unnecessary because the bow wake of the "Trooper" just pushed the Whaler aside.

Now Wayne was in the icy water with the "Trooper" leaving him and the wind blowing the Whaler away from him faster than he could swim. One of the crewmembers just happened to look out the rear porthole and noticed an orange dot in the water behind them. Not realizing what it was, he told the skipper they should probably go back and check it out. By the time they got back and fished Wayne out of the water, he was helpless and within a few minutes of death.

Incidentally, our department had recently issued day-glo orange float coats to us just prior to Wayne's accident. Up until then, we had been issued dark brown float coats. I honestly believe that, if Wayne had been wearing his brown coat, he may not have been noticed in the water. He was very lucky he was wearing the new orange float coat on that day.

Wayne must have had his fill of working on the salt water, because he soon transferred out of Kodiak.

*****

I was assigned a case once where a couple of elk were found dead on Afognak Island. I responded to the scene by Boston Whaler and our new Wildlife Officer, John Stimson, went along with me. We located the elk and found they been shot. One elk had died on a high bluff overlooking the ocean and the other one had gone over the bluff onto the rocks below.

John and I gutted out the elk and dug out the bullets.

We would later learn that they were 44-magnum caliber. We checked the area thoroughly for evidence and found only paper wrappers from "Three Musketeers" candy bars at one of the elk kill sites and on the beach where a small boat had recently been brought ashore. We placed the wrappers in evidence bags and headed across the water back to town. Sadly, the elk were very bloated and the meat unsalvageable.

John went back to the office while I stayed at the harbor in Kodiak and tried to come up with some information about any small boats that may have come in recently. I didn't turn up any information.

Later in the day, a man called the office and said that he had towed a small skiff back to Kodiak from Afognak. It had been beached and the pounding on the rocks had knocked a small hole in the bottom. He described the boat and said there were three men with it. They had to bail water out of their boat while he was towing it in.

I located the owner of the boat and learned who his two friends were. I noticed "Three Musketeer" candy bars around his home. When I mentioned them, he said he and his two friends were the Three Musketeers and it happens to be the best candy bar there is. I made arrangements to interview the three of them the following day at the trooper post.

Each man was interviewed separately and, fortunately, none of them were very bright. They loved to brag about the things they owned and things they did. When asked what type of firearms they owned, they each rattled off a long list and one of them mentioned a 44-magnum handgun.

When confronted with the ownership of the 44 magnum, the "Three Musketeers" wrappers at the scene of the dead elk and their boat being at the location, they became nervous and they gave conflicting stories about what they were doing over there. They still would not admit to shooting the two elk. The interviews were tape-recorded.

They turned their 44 magnum over to me and I ran a ballistics test on it. I filled a fifty-five gallon oil drum with water, stood on a short ladder and fired the gun down into the water. The bullets were undamaged and sent to the crime lab in Anchorage to be compared with the bullets we retrieved from the elk carcass'.

While the office secretary was typing up the interviews for me from the recorded tape, I heard her and a couple of our guys yucking it up much more than usual. I went over to see what all the laughter was about.

The tape I had used for the interviews was the same tape that I had at home for awhile and my kids had used it to record their favorite Muppets, Bert and Ernie. When I needed a tape, I grabbed that one. The tape now contained all the interviews, but right toward the end one suspect was describing being towed back to Kodiak and how they had to keep bailing water out of their boat. He said they were getting very tired and frustrated and he looked over at his partner and said...........at that point, his voice was cut out and Bert's (the Muppet) voice came on the tape saying, "Ernie pass me the hot dogs!" The remainder of the tape was all conversation between Bert and Ernie.

Luckily for me, this glaring error was toward the end of the interviews and would do no damage. I was not, however, looking forward to playing the tape in court. As it turned out, it wasn't necessary for me to play it. Justice won out in the end without our having to go through a court trial.

*****

Our Kodiak judge seemed a tad to lenient to those of us who made a habit of bringing poachers and violators to court. On one occasion, a man from one of the villages was tried before him for murder. The accused had caught his wife in bed with another man. The <u>next day</u> he took his shotgun and hunted the man down and shot him. He was found guilty of murder and given a very light sentence. The judge then told the convicted murderer that he could show up and start serving his sentence <u>after</u> the upcoming commercial fishing season.

*****

Kodiak Island is known the world over as the home of the giant brown bear. There are still plenty of nine-foot bears on the island and an occasional ten-footer. We had many hunting guides in the area and they stayed very busy with brown bear hunters from all over the world. A few of the hunters didn't stay long.

There was the one hunter who came to Kodiak from one of the "lower forty-eight" states and met his guide in town. As the guide was flying him out to the bear camp, he flew low over a large brown bear to show him to the hunter. The bear stood up on his hind legs and began swatting at the airplane with his front paws.

Well, that unsettled the hunter so badly that he decided he didn't want to be on the ground with one of those things. He made the guide bring him right back to town and left for home, forfeiting all the money he had paid for his airline ticket and the fifty percent deposit he had paid the guide.

*****

There were also the four bear hunters who came up from New York. Everything went fine with that group until they reached bear camp and realized that there was no telephone available to them at the camp. For some reason, they felt that they had to have a telephone nearby.

They came right back to town and into the trooper post. They wanted us to make the guide refund their deposit. Their only complaint was that they didn't know they would be without a telephone. They wouldn't say why they needed one so badly. They looked and acted like mobsters, which led to a lot of speculation in the office. We just told them we couldn't do anything about getting their money back, which was true.

*****

Two of the most admirable bear guides on Kodiak were Bill Pinnell and Morris Talifson. They were the old timers in the area. They began guiding for brown bear on Kodiak in 1949 and guided out of Olga Bay for 36 years. Their hunts were all fair chase. They hunted the old fashioned way...on foot without benefit of an airplane and still managed to maintain the best success record on the island. In the two years I was stationed in Kodiak, I only heard one complaint from their hunters. They said that Pinnell and Talifson apparently had no refrigeration when they first started guiding in the old days. They lived on Spam and cheese because it needed no refrigeration. "And they were still doing it in the mid-seventies!" By the time the hunt was over, the hunters didn't ever want to see another piece of Spam or cheese.

*****

One of the more interesting men I worked with on Kodiak was a great guy by the name of Dave Henley. He had a lot of admirable qualities, one of which was the superb physical condition he kept himself in. He had been a Kodiak rancher and a pilot for the Department for a lot of years.

He was working for Fish and Game in 1963 when he was assigned to bear control work. Kodiak Island had a few cattle ranches and the cattle were being regularly killed off by the big brown bears.

Dave used a Piper SuperCub with an M-1 Garand mounted on top to strafe the bears from the air. It fired with a button on the control stick and shot just over the propeller. It could be reloaded in flight and was extremely accurate.

This type of bear control was highly controversial and led to other solutions replacing the deadly aircraft. The complete story was written up in the August 1964, issue of Outdoor Life.

\*\*\*\*\*

One of our jobs as Wildlife Protection Officers was to conduct a "stake-out". We would take a little two-man camouflaged pup tent and secrete it in the alders. (They call it a two-man tent, but I think that only applies if the two men are very fond of each other.)

From our camp in the alders, we would spend the next week or so watching for suspected illegal activity such as bear poaching or commercial fishing violations in the bay. During these stakeouts, there were always bears around. They would come around the tent at night and give us an uneasy feeling. They would sniff, snort and growl while poking their noses onto the tent.

Our theory was that if we remained still, they would eventually go away. I found Kodiak brown bears to be good natured and not nearly as ornery as the interior grizzlies. Probably because of all the high protein salmon so readily available to them. They're pretty well fed.

Well, one of the other Wildlife Officers, John, was on one of these stakeouts when a bear came around one night poking the tent with his nose and snuffling about. After a while, John couldn't take it any longer and decided he'd better do something. He did. He hit the side of the tent and yelled. He scared the bear so badly that he jumped directly onto the tent and took off. John who was all tangled and twisted in the tent, thought the bear was still on top of him. He said he had nightmares about that night for a long time.

*****

I also had a bear incident that same year. I was dropped off in a bay where we suspected some boats had been coming in and robbing the creek (Netting salmon that are going up the creek to spawn). I hiked up to the only alder patch on the hillside overlooking the bay and set up my tent about fifteen feet inside the alders.

As I sat on the edge of the alders that evening, I saw a brown bear sow with two cubs down below me at the shoreline. I took some photos of them. As always, the cubs were unbelievably cute.

Moments after I had used up the last photo on that roll of

Author on Kodiak Island bear patrol.
(Photo by author with use of timer)

film, I saw a big brown bear boar coming around the edge of the alders in my direction. I moved back the fifteen feet to my camp and was digging through my backpack for another roll of film to photograph him going down to the water. What I didn't know was that he wasn't planning to go down to the water. He had walked along the edge of the alders to where I had been sitting and had turned into the alders heading my direction and was a mere fifteen feet away.

I was on my knees, bent over my pack and my department issued 350 Remington Magnum rifle was two feet away leaning against an alder branch. I quickly reached over with one hand, flicked the safety off and pulled the trigger with the rifle still leaning against the branch. The shot went straight up into the air. I then moved over to the rifle and racked another round into the chamber.

It wasn't necessary though, the bear had spun around and bolted out of the alders. I ran to the edge of the trees to see where he had gone. To my dismay, he had run back the direction from which he had come and was going back into the alders. The sow and two cubs had heard the shot and, not knowing where it came from, were running up the hill and went into the alder patch on the other side of me.

It was just starting to get dark. I went to bed in my little pup tent that night knowing that all four of those bears were in the same patch of brush with me. I dropped a couple of bullets into a small coffee can. As I slept that night, I would wake up every couple of hours and rattle that coffee can just to make sure those bears knew that I was still there.

That was the night that I slept with the bears.

*****

After working all those years around brown bears on Kodiak Island and on the Alaska Peninsula, I have had them within fifteen to twenty feet of me on several occasions, always accidentally. I would never intentionally let one get that close. I really didn't want my wife to become known as "Widow Carpenter".

I feel very lucky that I never had to kill a brown bear and that those close encounters worked out all right. Believe me when I say that a large part of it was luck. Firing warning shots is not always going to work. Each situation is entirely different and, if you fire a warning shot at the wrong bear, he could get to you before you could rack another bullet into the chamber.

There are times when it is necessary to kill a brown bear to protect your life or someone else's. I'm just glad I never had to. Even with all the opportunities I have had to take trophy brown bears, I have never shot one.

*****

One of those times that could have resulted in a dead bear was on Becharof Lake on the Alaska Peninsula where I was moose hunting with a very close friend of mine and his dad.

Bill Burke had lived on Kodiak since he was a teenager. He was a licensed plumber, a commercial fisherman and an excellent hunter. He and his wife, Donna, had become good friends of ours within a few weeks of our move to Kodiak. We enjoyed hunting and fishing together. We had also become very close to and very fond of Bill's dad who was known as "Pop". He was a wonderful old guy, gruff on the outside and kind hearted on the inside.

Bill and Pop had hunted Becharof Lake many times, but Pop was getting older and Bill and I wanted to get him over there once more on what would probably be his last Becharof hunt. Kodiak Airways dropped us off at the lake the day before moose season. We spent the remainder of that day setting up camp and getting ready for hunting the next day.

The camp was an old trapper's cabin with one wall entirely gone and a leaky roof. We had brought a large roll of Visqueen and used it to cover the roof and the missing side. The floor inside was part boards and part sand. We christened it the "Becharof Sand Palace". There was the frame of a kid's swing-set out in the weeds that would be perfect for hanging moose meat.

The next day, with the aid of a spotting scope, we saw a bull moose across the lake. We jumped into the rubber boat Bill had brought and fired up the motor. It's a long way across the lake. When we got there and started hunting the area, there turned out to be three bull moose. We got all three and had just enough time to gut them out by dark.

We went back early the next morning to pack the meat down the hill to the boat. Unfortunately, a big "brownie" had also found the carcasses and had plans for them. Pop had to stand guard with a rifle for us while Bill and I packed meat to the boat.

Anyone who had packed an Alaskan moose on their back will tell you that each moose represents five pack trips. We had fifteen trips to make from the kill site to the boat. All with a big brown bear standing in the alders close by and watching us closely.

We had left our two rifles in the boat so we could pack the meat. One of those times we had taken a load down, we saw the bear coming down the beach toward us looking very serious. Bill started up the outboard and ran at him with the boat while I, standing in the bow, fired shots into the gravel around him. He didn't seem very frightened, but he did turn around and move slowly away. He continued to watch us as we finished packing the rest of the moose down to the boat. When we left, he had enough moose entrails, hide, hair and hooves for a three-week "all-you-can-eat" buffet.

We hung the moose meat on the swing-set to cure. Later that day another bull moose walked through camp within fifty feet of the cabin while we stood and watched him for several minutes.

We had filled all three tags on the opening day of moose season. The problem was that we weren't due to be picked up by the plane for another week.

It began to rain and continued off and on all day every day. Each time it started raining, we would cover the meat with Visqueen, leaving room for air underneath. When the sun came out periodically, we would run out and uncover it. By the time we were due to be picked up, the weather socked in. For the next few days, either we were socked in at Becharof so they couldn't get into us or Kodiak was socked in so they couldn't get out of there.

Pop kept himself entertained by going outside, putting his mouth against the cabin and humming loudly. Bill and I would get all excited and run out the door, expecting to see an airplane.

Finally, one day, Kodiak Airways showed up. They took Bill back to town with our gear and part of the moose meat. They would be back in the morning to haul Pop and me out with the remainder of the meat.

That last night I was awakened by the sound of something scratching on the Visqueen over the swing set. I woke Pop up and whispered, "Pop, we've got a bear!" I said I'd turn the flashlight on him (through the Visqueen side of the cabin) and we both readied our rifles. I shined the light on the bear and saw him wheel around and take off running right past the front of the cabin. The bear was so big and heavy that, as he ran by, the ground shook and the cabin door rattled leading Pop to think that the bear was trying to come in through the door. I'll never forget the comical picture I have in my mind of Pop, standing on top of his sleeping bag in his long johns with his rifle aimed at the door, and his finger squeezing the trigger. I wish I hadn't opened my big mouth and said, "He's gone, Pop." I should have kept quiet just to see how many holes Pop would have put through that door.

*****

## Some Special People

There are three very special men I think of when I think of Kodiak Island.

Pop Burke was a wonderful old man, one in a million. I remember many times hearing Bill say to him in his own stylish way, "Yun's is a good Popper." Well, Pop, Yun's were a good Popper and a good friend. We all miss you. Rest in peace.

*****

Larry Carr went through the academy with me in 1973-74. He was very tough and very bright. He was fun to be around and well liked. Larry came out of the academy as a "blue shirt" and was assigned to Kodiak. His career was short lived. He died along with Frank Rodman, a "brown shirt", when their plane crashed into the sea off the coast of Cape Chiniak while they were making a medical rescue.

*****

John Stimson joined the "brown shirts" while I was in Kodiak and was an excellent officer. We worked together on many cases. John loved the sea and became very proficient with the larger boats.

In the winter of 1983 he was involved in a search and rescue by helicopter in poor weather conditions. The helicopter crashed leaving the pilot injured and John unharmed. The damage to the helicopter made it impossible for them to get to the emergency gear in the rear storage compartment. John cared for the injured pilot and sat in front of him all night protecting him from the elements. The pilot survived, but John died that night from exposure. He died a hero.

I was in Florida at the time of John's death and heard about it by phone. Linda attended the elaborate department funeral for me and was touched and impressed by the camaraderie of the department members.

*****

There is a Coast Guard base located just outside of the town of Kodiak. Occasionally they would run a winter survival course for their new people. The course was called "Cool School". It consisted of the Coast Guard flying the "students" out to a remote area and dropping them off where they would spend several days on their own.

Our department was asked if there was anyone interested in participating. Of course, I was.

There were two groups who would take part. One group was the young Coast Guard recruits who were relatively inexperienced in outdoor survival. Most of them were from other states, which made them unfamiliar with Alaska in general. There were about ten men in that group. I was asked to be the group leader.

The second group consisted of all high-ranking officers. They would be dropped off in the same general area, but away from us.

I was impressed with the two-hour class the Coast Guard presented to us before flying us out. They laid out the rules of the survival course and explained all the different food sources we could find and utilize. The only food we would have during the next few days was what we could find or catch. Each man would have to build his own individual shelter. The only items we were allowed to take with us were what we were issued. Those few items were things that you could expect to be able to salvage off of a wrecked aircraft. They searched us and confiscated several candy bars from a couple of the sneakier participants.

We were then flown out and dropped off on a remote bay. We were given our issued items which consisted of a small piece of silk parachute per man, some wire, one hatchet per group, some light line and a piece of metal which could be used for heating water. Water was no problem as we had about six inches of snow on the ground.

Our assignment was to build our shelters, secure food any way we could (except we were not allowed to kill or snare deer) and prepare three signal fires in a triangle

Nine foot Kodiak Brown Bear (Photo by author)

configuration, which could be quickly lit at a moment's notice. The Coast Guard would fly over us in three days. If we could get our signal fires lit quickly enough for them to be spotted by the aircraft personnel, they would land and pick us up. If the signal fires were not burning, the aircraft would keep going and would come back the next day. That would give us another chance to have our signal fires ready. Three fires in a triangle is a universal emergency signal. The group of officers had the same assignment.

I had a great bunch of guys with me. They were young, energetic and hard workers. We built our individual shelters using driftwood and dead branches. We covered that frame with heavy pine boughs for insulation and protection from the elements. We then stretched our small piece of parachute over the top of that. On the inside, we laid the fine tips of pine boughs to a depth of about a foot. That made a comfortable bed up off the cold ground.

We had no problem getting food. Thirty wire snares, over the three days, gave us about a dozen rabbits. We went out at low tide and picked up whatever we could find in the sand and on the rocks. We ate sea urchins, mussels, kelp and limpets, which are also called Chinese hats. Some of those were eaten raw and some were boiled. On those cold, wet days the hot broth left over from boiling the mussels and kelp in seawater really hit the spot.

We prepared our signal fires by stacking dry firewood in a teepee shape to a height of about eight or ten feet. Inside this stack, we placed a large amount of very fine and dry tinder. We kept a campfire going at all times, and arranged for three of our guys to each grab a stick out of the fire and use it to ignite the signal fires at the first sound of an approaching aircraft.

On the afternoon of the third day, the plane came and our fires were lit. It went very smoothly. We all had an enjoyable experience, learned a lot and were now about to be picked up.

The group of officers who were camped over a small hill from us must have had a lookout watching us, because as soon as our signal fires were lit, here they came. They came up to our fires, warmed themselves and waited to be picked up with us. Several of them had bad colds and appeared to be very sick.

Once we were delivered back at the Coast Guard base, we were interviewed in one large group about our experience. I learned a lot about people during that interview. I learned that people can get so spoiled from having others waiting on them that they lose the ability to do things for themselves. That seemed to be the case with the group of officers. Once they were dropped off at their survival site, instead of rolling up their sleeves and going to work like my guys did, they tended to stand around waiting for the others to do the work. They didn't take the time to build an adequate bough bed or weather tight shelter and nearly froze each night. They didn't feel like finding food and hadn't eaten much of anything during those three days. They didn't even bother to attempt building signal fires. They spent their entire time standing around a campfire trying to stay warm and, even then, argued with each other over who should go get more firewood.

Is it human nature for people, as they get more important, to become less self-sufficient? Do we get so used to having others wait on us that we can no longer take proper care of ourselves? It appears that way to me in this case.

I was very proud of the way my group worked and handled our situation. There is no doubt in my mind that if one of us had been with the officers' group, they would have expected us to do all the work while they stood by. That's pretty sad when you think about it.

\*\*\*\*\*

Linda, Darin, Chad and I stayed on Kodiak for two years. By then, we had gotten tired of the rain and were beginning to feel "island-bound". We put in for a transfer back to the mainland. We received confirmation of a temporary transfer to Anchorage and then on to Palmer as an opening in Palmer was expected. Just before our transfer, Linda and I both became allergic to shellfish, which is quite common in Kodiak. We had eaten so much shellfish during our two years there that we had finally reached our tolerance level. We have always been grateful that it didn't happen while we were living there.

Now…on to Anchorage and Palmer.

\*\*\*\*\*

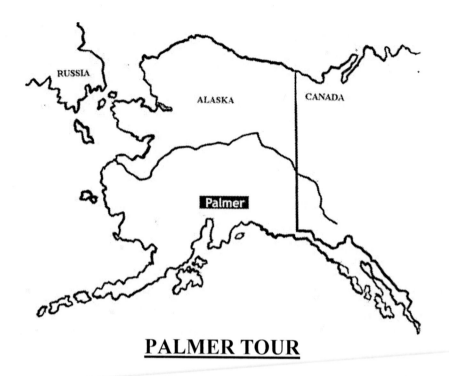

# PALMER TOUR

In the spring of 1977 my family and I left Kodiak and flew back to Michigan to visit family. We had ordered a new Chevrolet Blazer from the Chevy plant and picked it up while down there. We then bought a small travel trailer and started our trip back to Alaska with both of our mothers along. Fortunately, our mothers were long-time friends and the six of us had a great three-week trip coming back up.

We spent a couple of months in Anchorage while waiting for the position in Palmer to open up. Palmer is located in the Matanuska Valley about forty-five miles from Anchorage. We were making occasional trips out to the Valley to look for housing. Wasilla is another small town just ten miles from Palmer and we were also checking out in that area.

We found the house we wanted just five miles out of Wasilla and shortly afterward were transferred to Palmer.

The timing was perfect. Our house in Kodiak then sold and we were settled into our new surroundings.

Wasilla was a small quiet town with a population of less than a thousand in 1977. It was a good place to live and, if we needed anything from a bigger town, Anchorage was less than an hour away.

The patrol area for the Palmer post included approximately an eighty-mile stretch of the Glenn Highway. This portion of the Glenn Highway runs through the Matanuska River Valley and the scenery is spectacular.

There are two large glaciers visible from this stretch of highway, the Knik Glacier and the Matanuska Glacier. The Matanuska is one to which you can drive within a few feet.

The Knik Glacier is farther back from the highway and in order to patrol its surrounding area, we normally used four wheelers to cross the various creeks and drive up the gravel bars. There are lots of moose and mountain sheep in that area, making enforcement patrols a necessity.

As you follow the Matanuska River northward from Palmer, you will see majestic mountain ranges on both sides. The Chugach Mountains are on the east side and the Talkeetna Mountains are on the west. Both ranges are true wilderness areas and, because of their ruggedness, will remain wilderness for a long time to come.

The area I just described was only a fraction of our total patrol area, but it has some of the most incredible scenery. We also worked the Parks Highway, which included some of the most active fishing creeks around. In addition, there were numerous local roads and trails. We had a good variety of work to do.

In all, the Palmer area was a good one out of which to work. We would end up spending eleven years there.

*****

One morning while on foot patrol, I found a few drops of blood in the snow and traced them back to a freshly killed moose. It had been quartered and cached under a pile of spruce boughs. I notified my Sergeant and, thinking the poacher would probably be showing up that day to retrieve some of the meat, I went back to the kill site and staked it out.

I was warmly dressed and was very comfortable for an hour or so. As time went on, I grew cold and tired of standing still. I crouched and sat on the backs of my heels. Time dragged on. Several hours went by. It was almost completely dark and I was about to give up and hike back to the truck that was parked about a half mile away.

Suddenly, I saw the poacher walking toward the brush pile containing the moose carcass. He was pulling a small toboggan and had a dog with him. I waited until he actually removed some of the brush and placed a moose quarter on his toboggan before I stood up from a crouched position and yelled, "Don't move!" Well, he moved. He took off on a dead run with his dog beside him and left the toboggan behind.

I started after him, but after being in the freezing temperatures for so many hours and in a crouched position a lot of that time, I could barely move. It must have taken me fifty yards just to get limbered up again. He was running with a limp, but he had still outdistanced me. We continued to run until we almost reached Schrock Road, which was a main gravel road in the area. It was dark and I had lost him.

I hadn't expected to be out there that late and didn't have a flashlight with me. I would have to come back and try to pick up his tracks in the snow in the morning.

The next morning my sergeant and I were able to track the poacher to his cabin in the woods. After a period of denial, he admitted to the poaching and accepted his citation to court. The meat, as in all of these type cases, went to charity. The poacher had a stiff leg, which he was unable to bend. It was kind of an embarrassment to me that my sergeant knew that I had been outrun by a man with only one good leg.

\*\*\*\*\*

We received a report of a man who stopped at the site of a road-killed moose calf and threw it in the back of his pickup and drove off. The complainant had gotten the license plate number of the pickup. When the charity organization had shown up to salvage the moose, it was gone. I traced the violator through his license plate number and contacted him. I took the moose meat and "Dan" was cited into court.

Because "Dan" was so cooperative with me and the violation was a minor one, I advised the judge that leniency would be appropriate in this case. "Dan" was sentenced to pick up the next few road-killed moose and deliver them to the charities. He was very grateful to get off that lightly and stated so.

For the next month or so we would come home on occasion and find our driveway had been mysteriously plowed of snow. It occurred about four times and we had no idea who was doing it. One day while we were gone, our son stayed home. When we returned our driveway was, once again, mysteriously plowed. However, our son was able to describe the truck. It had been "Dan". I contacted him and he said he just wanted to do something for me, because I had shown faith in him and stood up for him in court. I told him it had been a nice thing for him to do, but it would be best if he discontinued plowing our drive.

*****

I came home one day with a moose calf whose mother had been struck and killed by a vehicle. The calf was only one day old and was snuggling up against her dead mother for comfort. Our kids named her "Bambi". (I think all moose calves are named either Bambi or Bullwinkle.)

Bambi became very attached to us, as we did to her, and she followed us around the property untethered like a puppy dog. She remained loose during the day to browse and was put in a shed at night for protection. She would run up the steps to our second story level and stare in the window at us hoping we would come out to play. We bought a calf bottle and raised her on goat's milk and limewater. She did great on that formula and could suck the two-quart bottle dry in under ten seconds. Supposedly, goat's milk was the next best thing to moose milk for her.

My mother visited us while we had Bambi and she enjoyed her immensely. Mom coaxed her into our living room. We didn't normally let her into the house (I mean Bambi, not Mom). Mom started feeding her Ritz crackers and Bambi decided she loved them.

Many friends and neighbors came by to see and photograph Bambi. Eventually, as the word spread, other people were coming by with their small children to show them the baby moose. They could actually walk up to her and pet her.

Author feeding moose calf "Bambi" her formula of goat's milk and limewater. (Photo by Linda Carpenter)

The plan was to care for her until late fall when she would be old enough to take care of herself and then release her into the wild. She would be released in a large moose reserve where no hunting was allowed; possibly up in Denali Park in the shadows of Mt. McKinley.

Sadly, Bambi developed pneumonia after getting soaked in a hard rain. The local veterinarian gave her a shot of antibiotics, but she died the next morning. One of our neighbors also had six Holstein calves die the same day from pneumonia. We all missed Bambi the moose.

*****

While on patrol, I would occasionally want to get a message to Linda, but dared not use the police radio for personal business. At times, a telephone was not available, so I devised a code. I had given Linda the nickname "Charlie" long before and I decided to use that as a code name. If I was going to be late for dinner, I would radio the dispatcher and ask her to call a number (which happened to be my home number) and, "Tell Charlie that I'll be an hour late for our appointment."

That worked great for several years until one day when I had asked the dispatcher to give "Charlie" a message. I was then out of my vehicle for a while, looking around the area just a short distance away. Upon returning to the vehicle, I heard one of the supervisors asking if anyone knew of my whereabouts. One of the troopers came on and said, "I just heard him on the radio asking the dispatcher to give a message to someone named Charlie. Then another trooper, who was a good friend of ours and knew that I sometimes called Linda "Charlie", came on the air. He said, "Yeah, Charlie's his wife."

I had to abandon that system and come up with another one.

*****

In March of 1978 my younger and better looking brother, Greg, moved up to Alaska from Michigan with his wife, Lucy. He had a degree in law enforcement and planned to enter that field. He soon went to work for the Palmer City Police Department from where he later retired as a first sergeant. He and Lucy still live in Palmer with their two sons, Jared and Preston.

*****

On August 14, 1978, Linda and I were blessed with a third son, Tyson. He was a welcome addition to our family and he gave the two older boys someone to pick on and torment.

*****

I was driving down the Knik Goose Bay Road out of Wasilla one day when a pickup, swerving back and forth across the center line and heading my direction, ran me off the road and onto the shoulder. I turned around and stopped the vehicle after chasing him a few miles.

The driver was drunk, argumentative and slightly resistant to arrest. I got him contained in handcuffs and transported him to the Palmer City Jail.

My brother, Greg, was on duty. He was the one to fingerprint and lock the drunk up after I did the initial booking and had left. The drunk carried on and on to Greg about what a S.O.B. Trooper Carpenter was. He had a lot of bad and nothing good to say about me. He then noticed Greg's nametag and said, "Carpenter? You're not the one who arrested me, are you?"

Greg said, "No, that was my brother."

The drunk shut up and remained quiet the rest of the night.

*****

Our two older sons, Darin and Chad, were active during this time with the organization, "Student Troopers". It gave them a chance to learn about the troopers' duties and be helpful to the Department. Chad, especially, got in a lot of helicopter time while assisting in search and rescues. He also helped out with some of the police training by playing the part of the "bad guy" in crime scenarios and Crime Stopper ads.

*****

While stationed in Palmer and living in Wasilla, I decided that there would be a big advantage, at times, to patrol my area by airplane. A lot of our hunters and fishermen were getting to and from the hunting and fishing areas by plane. I started my training in a Cessna 150 at the old Wasilla airstrip, which ran adjacent to, and only a few feet from the downtown store buildings. After receiving my license, I went in with a friend of mine and bought a Champ (tail dragger). I took my tail dragger instruction from Dick Williams who owned Williams Air Service on the Wasilla strip. I also obtained my float rating from him. Dick was also a career high school teacher, which made him especially talented as a flight instructor. He had a knack for getting information across to his students.

I began flying Super Cubs for the Department of Public Safety and was thoroughly enjoying it. I wanted to be a better pilot so I went to Daytona Beach, Florida, for more instrument training and obtained my commercial pilot license.

My partner and I sold our Champ and I then bought a 90 horsepower Champ with no electric. It was fun to fly because of the great performance it gave. The drawback was that I had to hand prop it to start it and I didn't like doing that with a non-pilot passenger sitting in the back seat. I eventually sold it and bought a Citabria.

*****

In the summer of 1977 the Department sent me to the small village of Emmonak near the mouth of the Yukon River to work the upcoming commercial fishery. I flew to Bethel and from there to Emmonak. Once there, I picked up a skiff, which would serve as my patrol vessel while I was there. The Department had also sent an aide to assist me with enforcement of the fishing regulations.

I had heard that in the past, our guys that were stationed there ended up with dysentery from the drinking water. The problem was that the villagers were dumping their honey buckets into the river in the area of where the drinking water came from. I wasn't about to take a chance on my aide or me getting sick so the first thing we did was to go to the local store. We bought a large trashcan and hauled it upstream until we found a clear water stream dumping into the Yukon. We filled our trashcan and that's what we used for drinking water during our stay. We did well and never got sick.

The Yukon River originates in northwest British Columbia, enters Alaska near the village of Eagle and runs the full width of Alaska where it then dumps into the Bering Sea. The Yukon's total length is 2,000 miles. This part of the Yukon River, near the mouth is two to three miles wide with salty, unclear water and is loaded with sandbars, some visible and some just under the water, making navigation a real challenge. It is not uncommon to see a boat stuck on the bottom.

Although the Yukon Delta has many channels (approximately 20), large boats can't use most of them because they're too shallow and are full of sandbars. They use the northernmost channel, which is still only a few feet deep at low tide.

*****

An interesting thing about migrating salmon is that the condition they are in when they enter their rivers depends on how long a trip upriver they are destined to make. Some of the salmon entering the mouth of the Yukon will end up spawning 1,000 miles upriver, 1,500 miles upriver and even 2,000 miles away in British Columbia. As you can well imagine, those salmon enter the Yukon in superb shape. They are some of the brightest and fattest salmon in the state.

*****

The people in Emmonak are Yupik Eskimo. They were warm and friendly with me and seemed very happy. I met a couple of men who were very talented at boat building and had a couple under construction. Emmonak had a community sauna where a hot fire was built and steam was generated by sprinkling water over the metal stove and rocks. The villagers, male and female alike, enjoyed their sauna. I like a good hot steam and could stay in longer than some of the locals. A favorite game of some of the tough old men was to build up the fire, douse the stove with lots of water and get the sauna as hot as possible to see who could outlast the others.

*****

The commercial fishing violations on the lower Yukon varied, but, if I remember right, the most common violation was fishing on days when the season was closed. Everyone was cooperative when it came to accepting their citations to court and showing up.

Court in Emmonak was a whole new experience in itself. The courthouse was a pre-fab unit and the jail cell was one of the closets with a small square hole rough-cut in the door about head high. The magistrate was a very pretty and professional lady who, as it turned out, was related to nearly everyone in the village, including the violators I brought in to her court.

The jailer was a small wrinkled-faced man with no teeth. He seemed to take immense pleasure in keeping the guys in the closet (jail cell) in line. He would open the closet door, yell something at them in Yupik and close the door. Then he'd turn around with his arms folded across his chest and a big toothless grin on his face.

I played the parts of the arresting officer, the prosecutor, and the court secretary. The magistrate had asked me to write down the court proceedings for her.

Each violation was presented and court kind of went this way: I would stand up and state the prosecutions case of the violation and all the surrounding facts and evidence. The magistrate and the defendant would then carry on a conversation in Yupik (which was Greek to me). The magistrate would then turn to me and explain what all had been said and done. Of course, I had to take her word for it and write everything down as she told me. I felt that she was a fair magistrate and gave appropriate fines and sentences. I would have felt better about what was actually said, however, if everyone hadn't left in such a jovial mood.

*****

One of the Palmer Fish and Game biologists called me one day and said he had a report of an injured moose with a broken leg out on the flats. I told him I'd pick him up and go with him. We found a cow moose with the broken leg. We wanted to get a closer look at the leg to see if it was broken badly enough to require shooting her. Some breaks are not all that severe and, if given a chance to heal, will build a calcium deposit around the break and make it usable again. Sometimes the moose will end up with a stiff leg, unable to bend it, but we have found them the next season with a large calcium deposit around the break and getting around well. Sometimes they'll even have new calves with them.

We got close enough to determine that this moose's leg would probably heal. About that same time, she decided we were up to no good and charged us. Jack and I ran and found safety behind a tree. I learned that day that a moose can run just about as fast on three legs as they can on four.

*****

One fall, a fellow Wildlife Officer and I were assigned to work the moose hunt on the Innoko River with the Super Cub on floats. John Knudsen was a good pilot and handled the Cub well.

The Innoko River is near the west coast of Alaska, runs parallel to the Yukon River and then dumps into the Yukon River just below the native village of Shageluk. It is an area well known for giant moose with record-book antlers.

At one point, John and I decided to take a break from patrolling and stretch our legs on a large gravel bar. As we walked along, we checked out the various rocks on the bar. Seeing one dark and unusual rock I poked at it with my boot. It didn't keep my attention and I continued on. John came along and poked the rock with his toe. He picked it up and found it to be a fossilized mammoth tooth about three inches wide and six inches long. We started looking closer at the gravel bar and John found a large stone spearhead while I found a large stone ulu (crescent-shaped knife). Both were hand tooled out of rock and were in perfect condition. Then it was time to get back to work.

We were told that someone wanted to file a complaint against a guide who took a moose on the same day he was airborne (a serious violation in Alaska). We located the complainants on the river. One turned out to be with the National Audubon Society while the other two, if I remember right, were with U.S. Fish and Wildlife. If you're going to commit a violation, they are not the guys you want

91

to see you doing it. They were great witnesses and had all the details for us. They related the story as follows.

One of the U.S. Fish and Wildlife guys; we'll call him "Gary", had spotted a large bull moose and was tracking him. Gary actually removed his clothes and, holding them up out of the water along with his rifle, swam across the cold Innoko River to the other side. There he got dressed and continued his stalk. As he was getting close to the moose, he saw a guide fly overhead, land and let out the assistant guide and a hunter. The assistant guide and hunter were racing to beat Gary to the moose. When he realized that the hunter was going to be too slow, the assistant guide shot the moose for the hunter. Imagine how mad Gary was after all his effort.

John and I located and contacted the guide at his hunting camp. Upon completion of the interviews, we seized the guide's airplane. It was a Cessna 185 on floats, probably worth about $80,000 new. One of our officers came down and checked out the airworthiness of the 185. He then flew it back to our hangar on Lake Hood in Anchorage. John and I flew our Cub back to McGrath.

We left McGrath en route to Anchorage and shortly ran into heavy fog. We turned around, but found that it had socked in behind us also. We had no choice—we put it down on the first gravel bar we came to. We built a campfire to stay warm and, while walking around, John found a box of military rations. It contained ham, cheese, candy, etc. I've never seen anyone as lucky as John. After a few hours, the fog lifted and we headed home. It was always a good feeling to have returned from those trips safely.

*****

In the summer of 1983, I was assigned to take the Super Cub to Yakutat and work the commercial fishery off the beaches. Yakutat was a great place to fly out of and with the narrow sandy beach running along the coastline there was always a place to land. The system of traffic control there worked quite well. The sandy beach was used like a centerline on a highway. Any eastbound aircraft would fly out over the water with the beach off the left wing tip. Any westbound aircraft would fly over the brush with the beach off his left wing tip. That system, along with the fact that there was almost no other light aircraft in the area, made it fairly safe to fly down the coast even on days when it was too foggy to fly inland. I was able to fly every day and was putting in twelve to eighteen hours each day patrolling the area and working the fishery.

The beaches were lined with strawberry plants and an occasional brown bear could be seen enjoying the super sweet berries. There are a lot of brown bears in the Yakutat area.

Less than an hour's flight east of Yakutat is an area called Dry Bay. There is a long gravel airstrip there where I had a white wall-tent and a three-wheeler to use in the fishery patrol in conjunction with the Super Cub. That strip was also used by a DC-3 flying out of Yakutat. They would land at the Dry Bay strip and pick up a large load of salmon from the fishermen and fly it back to Yakutat.

One particular day, I was working out of Dry Bay when the DC-3 was coming in. There was thick brush lining both sides of the runway with a couple of openings cut through it allowing access to the runway. I taxied up to the brush and through the opening to the runway. From there, I had a clear

Preparing Super Cub for Yakutat assignment.
(Photo by Linda Carpenter)

view of the approaches. I saw the DC-3 coming in for a landing. It was a complete surprise, as I had not heard any radio transmission from them.

As it was later learned, they had mistakenly used the radio frequency commonly used for rural airstrips instead of Dry Bay's assigned frequency.

I was several feet from the edge of the runway, but felt I should get further back to leave lots of room for them. I shut off the engine, jumped out and pushed my Cub back a few feet further from the runway. I got back in and started the engine up again.

The brush blocked my view of the DC-3's landing and rolling out, but suddenly I saw the wing tip come out over the brush and swinging in a wide arc toward me. Instead of turning around in the wide area for that purpose just ahead of them, they apparently didn't know I was there and were turning around right in front of me. They hadn't heard my transmissions because they were on the wrong frequency. The large metal wing tip swung over my cowling, and my spinning propeller chewed the hell out of the underside of it. Of course, it didn't do my prop any good either. It broke off about eight inches of one of the tips. The DC-3 pilot felt pretty sheepish. I dug out my "hundred mile an hour" tape (silver duct tape) and we taped up their wing. After the pilot and copilot loaded their salmon, I rode back to Yakutat with them.

The Department investigated and determined that the DC-3 pilot was responsible for the incident. They shipped down a new prop, which I installed on the Cub, and I continued my commercial fishery patrols. That was the first and last time I was ever run over by a DC-3. That prop and the prop I damaged a year later on Montague Island were the only damage I ever did to an aircraft in all the time I flew for the Department or for myself. I was very lucky in that respect.

*****

While I was in Yakutat, Linda, Chad and Ty flew down to spend some time with me. We stayed in an empty house, which would be state housing for the future Fish and Wildlife Trooper and slept on the floor. I took them over to show them the office and jail. They were not impressed. The office was just an old office and the jail was a cell in the corner of the office built out of two-by-fours. The gaps between the upright two-by-fours were so wide that Chad, who was sixteen years old, could squeeze through them and spent several minutes doing it for our amusement. There wasn't anything in the cell except for an old overstuffed chair.

I took enough time off while they were there for us to see some of the countryside and some brown bears up close. Then it was time for them to return home and for me to go back to my twelve to eighteen hour workdays.

*****

They say everyone has their "fifteen minutes of fame". I guess mine came in March of 1984. I was flying the Super Cub on a patrol out of Palmer over the Knik Glacier/Coghill Lake area. From there, in a southeast direction, several islands are visible out in the Prince William Sound. Of these islands, one was Montague.

Montague Island is a long, narrow island of about fifty miles by about ten miles. It is mountainous with some of of its peaks reaching three thousand feet. It is heavily treed

Author and his son, Ty, in Yakutat's 2" x 4" jail cell.
(Photo by Linda Carpenter)

and holds a large number of Sitka black-tailed deer. There are also sea lions and a wide variety of sea birds. Numerous brown bear wander the island and usually frequent the salmon spawning streams during late summer.

I remembered that, during one of my coffee discussion groups at the Kashim restaurant, several pilots mentioned hearing of hunters flying to Montague to poach brown bears. I radioed dispatch and advised them of my plans to check out the area. I heard a response of "10-4". Unknown to me at that time, Anchorage dispatch did not receive my transmission or received it garbled and was actually "10-4ing" someone else. I flew over the island and checked the beaches for aircraft, there were none.

By then, I badly needed to take a leak and landed on one of the beaches. Before landing and stopping on any questionable beach, proper procedure is to touch down and, without stopping, continue to roll along the beach and lift off again. This gives you a chance to feel the integrity of the sand or gravel and tell whether it is solid enough to come to a complete stop. Sometimes we take a shortcut if we're confident that the surface is solid. I took the shortcut. As I landed and was rolling along the beach at a slow speed it felt fine. Instead of slowing down a little more before taking off again, I just brought the plane to a stop. Unfortunately, I hit a soft spot and, just before coming to a stop, the nose of the plane tipped down and the tips of the propeller struck the gravel. Both prop tips were curled, making the Cub unflyable. I was able to taxi, but the beach was so soft I knew I would never be able to get up enough speed to lift off without bigger tires, even with an undamaged prop. It takes a little more runway to get off than it takes to land. I continued to taxi and maneuver until I had the Cub above the high tide line and in a position for takeoff. Now all I had to do was to make sure our department pilots found me. With big tires and a new prop, I would be able to fly this bird out of there.

I turned on my ELT (emergency locator transmitter). Then I picked up a lot of colorful flotsam and jetsam from the water's edge and spread it around the beach as a visual aid. There were a couple of bright colored rubber buoys along with lots of bright yellow rope. There was also a white plastic milk crate and lots of other colorful items that had drifted up onto the beach. In addition, I had a couple rolls of surveyors ribbon with which I decorated the area. It would only be a short time now before I was reported overdue and my partners would be there. I still didn't know that my radio message to dispatch had been somewhat garbled by my position over the mountains and they did not know my location. The Department pilots were out in full force early the next morning searching the entire area for me along with the Air Force and Coast Guard. Since I had been reported overdue, Linda had lots of company and support from family, friends and neighbors. She, herself, felt that I could take care of myself if I was down somewhere and had no doubts that I was all right. She's a strong woman.

Connie Rodesky, our neighbor across the road from us, lived alone and was very dear to us. She was quite concerned for my safety at first, but on the second day a moose walked up to her house and looked into her window at her. She said the moose looked so calm and peaceful, that she felt it was there to let her know I was all right. She told Linda she knew everything was okay and quit worrying after her visit from the moose.

I spent two nights in my sleeping bag under the wing of the Super Cub. Food was no problem as I had plenty of freeze-dried and some powdered items such as soup and hot chocolate, probably enough for two to three weeks. There was a fresh water lake and creek up the beach and a short distance into the woods. I couldn't figure out where my guys were though. It seemed that they should have been there long before now. My brother, Greg flew with my friend and fellow trooper, Garland Dobson to join the search. Our oldest son, Darin was scheduled to fly with another friend. Finally, the third day, the Air Force helicopter picked up my ELT signal. They were in a large plane, which couldn't make a beach landing so they headed back to their base for a helicopter. Meanwhile, the U.S. Coast Guard landed with their helicopter. They gave me doughnuts and coffee and one of their sack lunches that they are famous for giving to rescuees. Then they left me there, explaining that, since the Air Force were the ones to find me, they get the honor and the publicity of hauling me back. The Air Force helicopter arrived and transported me to Elmendorf Air Force Base. I was grateful to both branches of the service. It was unfortunate that my radio message was not received or was misunderstood and the Coast Guard and Air Force and our troops had to be called out at all.

I later learned that Montague Island was supposed to be worked by our Cordova post instead of the Palmer Post. I was contacted at the trooper post by a popular newscaster from Anchorage and interviewed. When he asked me why I landed there, I said, "Mother Nature called and I had to land somewhere. I just picked the wrong beach." The interview was on all three Anchorage channels that night. I was given a couple of weeks off without pay for being outside my patrol area. I didn't sit around wasting time during my unplanned vacation. I got our house painted and a greenhouse built.

Unfortunately, word of the Montague incident got back to our hometown newspaper in Michigan. An old high school buddy in Denver, Colorado, received a copy of the hometown paper with my story in it. He still won't let me forget it to this day.

*****

Each spring, the Department of Public Safety sent a group of Fish and Wildlife Troopers out to the Alaska Peninsula to work the various guide areas during brown bear season. Sometimes they sent a few, other times there would be more of us. One thing was for sure, there would be some interesting events occurring each year.

The wind could be incredibly strong on the Peninsula. I remember one day departing the King Salmon airport with other troops in several Super Cubs. There was a severe cross wind making it impossible to safely take off down the runway. We taxied out to the runway and took off across the width of the strip. It doesn't take much distance to get a Cub off the ground in a strong head wind.

The pumice patches, which are scattered throughout the Alaska Peninsula, made ideal airstrips. We used them on a regular basis. In a strong wind, the cub could take off and land vertically, much like a helicopter.

I remember one particular evening my partner and I were coming in to the state cabin on Sandy River. The wind was picking up and we were glad to be back on the ground. Our tie down was a heavy steel cable secured to anchors buried in the ground. We also normally tied down the tail wheel. After hitting the sack that night, we woke up to

Sandy River cabin with aviation fuel cans stacked along side and the dependable 7056. (Photo by author)

stronger winds and heavy rain. We jumped out of bed and checked on the plane. It was trying to fly without us and was pulling our tie down cable out of the ground. We had visions of the wind blowing our plane away and destroying it. Our adrenaline was up. We dug holes for the front tires to lower the angle of attack. We rounded up seven or eight five-gallon cans of fuel and tied them to the wing struts. When we saw that wasn't going to be enough to hold it down, we grabbed on to the ropes and held on. There we were, in a rainstorm and high winds, hanging on to a plane that was trying to mutiny. I don't know how long that went on, but it sure seemed like a long time to me before the wind died down. Anything was better than having to explain how we lost the state airplane.

*****

The Sandy River cabin was a real piece of work. It had been built by a Fish and Game employee who towered in height over others and who decided the cabin should be built to fit him. It was built strong and solid and was a haven in severe weather. However, the door was six inches taller than normal and the windows were high enough that we had to stand on a box to see out of them. The kitchen counter was so high that we had our elbows up over our heads while flipping our eggs and pancakes. The ceiling rafters and roof were much higher than normal. Moving around in there made us feel like "Alice in Wonderland" during her small phase.

The outhouse, about fifty feet away, was even more weird. The seat was so high and wide that, while using it, our feet dangled about two feet off the floor. Incidentally, the slivered boards on the outside of the outhouse were covered with brown bear fur. That helped us decide to always take our rifles with us to the can.

*****

During the same Alaska Peninsula assignment, I was flying with that same partner and we were going to drop off a package to one of our guys who had been out on stakeout for a long period of time by himself. I was riding in the back seat of the Super Cub. Roy was flying. Since we knew Mike's stakeout position, we were able to fly directly to him. Airborne guides or hunters would not have noticed his hidden camp.

We had a big treat for him. We had brought a letter from his wife back home and the biggest, juiciest steak we could find. We knew he'd appreciate the steak after eating freeze-dried food for a week or two.

We couldn't land at his camp because of the terrain so we would have to make an air drop. That was no problem—-we had done it lots of times. We set up our approach for low and slow. As we neared his camp, Mike was out in front of his tent waving to us. We felt really good knowing that we were about to make his day for him.

Roy flew a flight line that would put Mike and his tent just off our left wing. I was holding the precious cargo in a specially wrapped package out the left window ready to be dropped. At the perfect instant, Roy said, "Now!" I released the package and watched as it went down toward the grateful friend below. Down…down…down and right into the river! Mike started chasing it downstream. We made a couple of circles, helpless to be of any assistance to him. When we left to return to our cabin, Mike was still running downstream, pausing only long enough to shake an occasional fist at us.

*****

While patrolling the west coastline of the Alaska Peninsula, it was fairly common to see a dead walrus on the beach below. If the beach was landable, we'd land to check the walrus out to see if it had been shot or died of other causes. Sometimes the carcass had been found by someone else and the ivory tusks would be gone. If the tusks were still there we had to leave them, because it was against department policy to transport the tusks in a department plane.

The oosik (penis bone) was also a valuable trophy. An adult walrus is twelve feet long and weighs up to 3,000 pounds. His sizable penis is in constant erection because of the foot and a half to two foot long penis bone. The oosik is often salvaged along with the tusks and is a great conversation piece. Although we do own a couple of oosiks, I don't think I'd ever have the heart to cut one off of those impressive mammals

*****

In the spring of 1988 I was assigned to take a hideout camp up into the mountains northwest of Anchorage and keep watch on a valley in which we suspected some illegal grizzly bear hunting activities by aircraft. My partner took me over in the helicopter so we wouldn't be leaving telltale ski tracks in the snow to alert the hunters that we were around. After being dropped off, I brushed away the helicopter tracks and my boot prints with an evergreen branch. I set up my tent and tied a white bed sheet over it for camouflage. I was located in the trees on a ridge overlooking the valley and a huge glacier. Because of the trees, there were areas I could walk to without my tracks being seen from the air. I was to be there for four days.

I was very lucky with the weather. It was beautifully sunny and warm. This land of ice and snow was spectacular. I found a point on the ridge, which was strategically located with an ideal view of the valley and the glacier. I was able to sit there in the sun, read a book and keep my eyes and ears alert for any activity. It was so warm those four days that I had stripped off my jacket and shirt and sat there in my tee shirt soaking up the rays of the sun reflecting off the glistening white snow. I snowshoed a couple of times a day for exercise in areas where my tracks would be hidden.

There wasn't any activity in the valley. Our information must not have been as good as we had originally thought. By the end of the fourth day I had developed a dark tan on my arms, neck and face. I was also part way through my book for the second time. I was not picked up as expected and it was now snowing. It continued to snow for the next three days. I had run out of food on the morning of my sixth day. I was still able to heat water for drinking. My partner was unable to get through the weather to me.

There was no urgent need for me to get out. I could hold out for another couple of days except that Linda and I were to leave in a couple of days for Hawaii. I could just imagine her basking in Hawaii with me stranded in this snowstorm. Trying to remain optimistic, I counted my blessings. I had plenty of snow to melt for hot water and with being well versed in wood lore, I could start a roaring campfire with nothing more than a few twigs, a gallon of white gas and a box of matches. I also had a good book, which I was getting to know very well by now. It was a big thick book called "Hostage to Fortune" by Ernest K. Gann. So far, I had read it two and a half times. It's a true story about a soldier of fortune who led one of the most interesting lives I've ever read about. The last I knew he was living in the San Juan Islands. If you like adventure, read it. It's good.

Anyway, to make a long story short, my partner was able to get in and pull me out on the seventh day. Linda and I caught our flight to Hawaii and I had the goofiest looking farmer's tan over there with my swimsuit on. I had dark arms, neck and face. The rest of me looked like a beached beluga whale. The Hawaiians and Californians would come up and say, "Are you from Alaska?" They could always spot an Alaskan by the pale white skin and sometimes by the tee shirt Alaskans wear over there that says "Alaskans don't tan, they thaw".

*****

Robert Service's popular verses were of special comfort on many a lonely night. My favorites of his are from "The Shooting of Dan McGrew", maybe because they remind me of the situations I have been in such as the previous stakeout.

"Were you ever out in the Great Alone, when the moon was awful clear,
And the icy mountains hemmed you in with a silence you most could hear;
With only the howl of a timber wolf, and you camped there in the cold,
A half-dead thing in a stark, dead world, clean mad for the muck called gold;

While high overhead, green, yellow and red, the North
Lights swept in bars?-
Then you've a hunch what the music meant…hunger and
night and the stars.
And hunger not of the belly kind, that's banished with
bacon and beans,
But the gnawing hunger of lonely men for a home and all
that it means;
For a fireside far from the cares that are, four walls and a
roof above;
But oh! So cramful of cozy joy, and crowned with a
woman's love—-
A woman dearer than all the world, and true as Heaven is
true.—-"

*****

Bristol Bay is one of the most productive salmon
fisheries in the State. Certainly, the most money is
expended and made there. Bristol Bay is part of the Bering
Sea, which is that northern portion of the Pacific Ocean
between Alaska and Russia. At one point, in the Nome and
Kotzebue area, there is only a fifty mile separation between
the two countries. The Bering Sea reaches depths of up to
13,000 feet while the Bristol Bay portion of it is relatively
shallow and gets extremely rough.

The fishery covers such a large area and involves so
many boats that adequate enforcement coverage requires
many "Fish and Wildlife" and "Fish and Game" personnel
and many patrol vessels. Fish and Game personnel are the
biologists while Fish and Wildlife enforces the fish and
game laws and regulations.

It became routine for me to be sent out to Bristol Bay
along with several other troopers to work the commercial

fishery. What a circus that was! There was so much competition between the fishermen that it was not unheard of for them to shoot at each other or ram each other's boats. Our patrol vessels normally included the 110-foot "Vigilant", the 60-foot "Trooper" and various Boston Whalers and rubber Coast Guard-type skiffs. Rainy, foggy weather with rough seas was the norm. Some days the seas were so rough that we traveled as many miles up and down as we did ahead.

Boarding the fishing boats from our patrol boats became a slippery, dangerous challenge in rough seas. With both boats bobbing up and down six or eight feet in the air, one going up while the other was coming down, the timing for stepping off one and onto the other had to be perfect. Of course, it wasn't always timed perfectly, and the results could be anything from embarrassing to painful.

The violations we were watching for were fishing without licenses, permits or proper boat paperwork. We watched for boats fishing closed waters or during closed season. The seasons opened and closed at certain times on certain days. A lot of extra fish, meaning extra money, could be gained by fishing early or late at the expense of the other boats. A boat caught fishing in closed waters or during closed season could lose his entire catch of fish on board. The fines paid for these violations were large and the money went back into the state funds.

On one occasion, I was in a small metal patrol boat with another trooper. We had been working the Goodnews Bay area. On our way back to Dillingham, we came across an immense flow of broken ice, which had flowed out of the Nushagak and Kvichak Rivers and was lying just off the mouths. We entered the ice flow and tried to push and maneuver our way through. We passed cakes of ice with walrus sitting and watching us, obviously wondering about our sanity. We eventually got through the ice jam and made it into the Dillingham harbor.

The Dillingham harbor is unique in that it goes dry at low tide. That makes it necessary to enter or exit the harbor at or near high tide. As the tidal waters flow out, the boats settle lower and lower until they are sitting firmly on the mud. There's no way to leave then until the next high tide. I assume there have been no changes and the harbor is still that way today.

*****

Occasionally arguments between fishermen turn violent and it falls upon our shoulders to interfere for the purpose of preventing further violence or investigating the damage already done. One of those incidents occurred during a Bristol Bay commercial fishing patrol.

Another trooper and I were in the wheelhouse of the patrol vessel "Vigilant" when we received a radio transmission requiring immediate action. Three set net fishermen had a camp and a set net site on the beach. One of those individuals had reported troubles and arguments between his two partners. While he was at camp and they were down at the beach, he thought he had heard a shot. Only one of his partners came back saying the other one had quit and left, on foot, for the nearest village. The third partner suspected foul play. He got out of there and caught a flight back to King Salmon.

Carl and I were dropped off on the beach by skiff. We walked down the beach toward where we knew the set net site to be. We found an area in the sand that had been disturbed as if something may have been buried there. A short distance away we saw a man working a net. He resembled the description we had been given of the suspect.

We contacted the suspect and determined his identity, saying nothing about the disturbed area of sand we had seen. He gave us his account of what had occurred and said his partner had walked off down the beach southbound.

There was a trooper plane from King Salmon en route to our location. Upon its arrival, we walked over to the area we thought may have held the missing man's body. Sure enough, it was a shallow grave. Carl and I then recontacted the suspect and placed him under arrest. He said that he and the victim had gotten into a fight and, since the other guy was bigger and stronger than him, he shot him. We put him in the plane and shipped him back to King Salmon.

We knew he had a 44 magnum and belt with holster and we wanted badly to find it. It could make the difference between a successful prosecution and an acquittal. We had found 44 ammo in the camp tent. By wading through the surf, I located the holster and belt with ammo in the belt. We feared the gun was possibly lost in the ocean. I waded through the surf as long as I could stand the cold water, but never found the gun.

Special investigators were en route to the scene by aircraft and would spend as much time as necessary to do a thorough search.

While waiting for the arrival of the investigators, Carl and I were guarding the areas of the camp and the beach to prevent any disturbance to those areas. I decided I had to answer the call of nature. I wandered out onto the other side of a sand dune, away from the beach, and made a deposit into a small hole in the sand. I neatly covered it with sand and went back to my guard duty. The investigators arrived,

Carl and I briefed them and left to go back to the "Vigilant" and resume our commercial fishery patrol.

After our leaving, a very sad and tragic event occurred. The investigators had brought along a metal detector. With it they hoped to find the missing gun, which was vital for our evidence. They used the metal detector to scour the beach, the camp area and the surrounding sand dunes.

One of the investigators followed foot tracks and spotted an area in the sand dunes where something had obviously recently been buried. Something about the size of a handgun! He was excited. His heart rate increased. He knew he had found what they were looking for. He dropped to his knees and began digging with his hands. He called out to his partner, "I think I've found it!" He continued digging with his hands. Suddenly, he grabbed onto the contents of the sand hole. It wasn't the gun. It was what I had left behind and so carefully buried. I understand that, to this day, he still eats his "Big Mac's" with gloves on.

The gun was later found buried in the dunes with the use of the metal detector. I met with the suspect in court in Dillingham later where he pled guilty to the charge of murder.

*****

One of the more enjoyable aspects of Fish and Wildlife Protection is working undercover. Sometimes we worked covert operations in major cases involving big game and guides. Other times we worked covertly in minor violations such as sport fishing.

We seldom worked covertly as our main objective was to be highly visible and prevent as many violations from occurring as possible. At the same time, we were not naive.

We knew that violations took place before and after we arrived on the scene in full uniform. Everyone who was fishing illegally would behave until we left the area and then continue whatever they were doing. By working in plain clothes occasionally, and catching violators, people tend to remain more honest because they don't know whether the person fishing near them is a legitimate fisherman or a trooper.

One day, while working in plain clothes on Fish Creek out of Wasilla and carrying a fishing pole, I saw a man intentionally snag a salmon. Now he was reeling it in. I slowly waded over to him. The fish was putting up a good fight. He handed me a net and said, "Here, net him for me, will ya?"

I said, "I don't think you can keep him, he's snagged in the side."

"Don't worry about it. There's no game wardens around here," he responded.

I netted the salmon, removed the hook and released him. The fisherman was furious. When I showed him my badge and hauled out my ticket book, he deflated while the other fishermen cheered and applauded.

*****

There was another time that I received a standing ovation while in plain clothes. It was on the Little Susitna River near Willow. There is a railroad trestle that crosses over the river and it's a popular fishing spot. I walked down the tracks to the river and saw a large group of fishermen. I was carrying a fishing pole and a tackle box.

There was one man standing on the trestle overlooking the river. I stood beside him to watch the people below.

There was a man on the bank below who was trying to snag a salmon. The man up on the trestle with me was the lookout for him and was trying to help him snag a fish. The guy below would cast out into the river and start slowly reeling the lure in. The guy on the trestle would coach him as we could see the fish much better than those below. He would say to his partner below, "Faster, faster, okay, now slow down and jerk!" At that time, the guy below would jerk his line as hard as he could. Fortunately, they were not very good at this and had not been successful.

The other fishermen were getting visibly agitated with these two obnoxious drunks and were muttering to each other. They were afraid to confront them, however, for fear of physical violence. I talked to the guy on the trestle to get an admission that he knew snagging was illegal. I then identified myself and took him down to his partner. When I started writing citations to these two guys, the two-dozen or so other fishermen laid their poles down and started clapping and cheering.

At that time, our post policy was to give warnings for attempted snagging and write citations to only those who actually snag a fish. Because of the special circumstances of this particular case, I elected to write citations. I wrote up the guy on the bank for "attempted snagging." We didn't have a regulation covering what the guy on the trestle was doing so I wrote him up for "assisting in attempting to snag". I was hoping he wouldn't fight it in court. He didn't. They both paid their fines. They had been very embarrassed that day on the river by the cheering and laughter of the crowd and I noticed they left the area when I did.

*****

The Matanuska and Susitna Valleys were inundated each winter with moose coming down out of the mountains to escape the deep snow. Unfortunately, the results were that many were killed by cars and trains. It was not uncommon for a few hundred to be killed over the period of a winter. The meat from the train kills was, of course, mostly unsalvageable. However the road kills were salvaged and donated to charity. There were many nights where we had three or four moose hit on the highways. Part of my job was to respond to these road hits, make sure the moose was going to survive or else make sure it was dead and salvaged. A lot of them were seriously injured with broken legs or other injuries and had to be dispatched (shot) with a twelve-gauge slug, usually behind the ear. There was nothing pleasurable about shooting moose under those circumstances. But, it had to be done. In my eleven years in Palmer, I probably had to shoot approximately a hundred injured moose.

*****

About fifteen miles out of Wasilla, off the Knik Goose Bay road, Fish Creek dumps into the Cook Inlet. Along the coastline within a mile or two of the mouth of Fish Creek we occasionally found illegal gill nets set to snare salmon en route to Fish Creek. Sometimes we caught the violators at the scene, but often they were either hidden in the brush or gone.

One night in particular, I located an illegal net fishing and decided to wait and watch for the poachers to return and pick the fish out of the net. I hid the truck in the trees and waited in the brush. I started developing uneasy feelings. Intuition, if you will. This situation, which was a repeat of several others, just didn't feel the same. I felt like I should have a back up.

I drove over to the home of my sergeant, Leon Steele, and picked him up. We went back and waited. Later that night a car drove in with three men in it. They got out and checked their net. When they pulled it back up on the beach, we surprised them. They ran. Leon yelled, "Stop or I'll shoot!"

They turned around, came back and we placed them in handcuffs.

One of our prisoners said he had to take a leak really bad. Leon removed his handcuffs and he did his thing. I saw him drop a slip of paper and, after Leon placed him back in cuffs, I went over and picked up the paper. It appeared to be a slip of cocaine. I asked him about it and he denied dropping it. I saved it for evidence and we started marching them back to our patrol vehicle. It was hidden quite a ways away.

We decided that, instead of walking them all the way back, it might be better if Leon stood guard over them while I hurried on ahead and brought the vehicle to them. I didn't like the idea really of leaving my partner with three prisoners, so as soon as I got out of sight, I started jogging toward our vehicle. Immediately, I heard Leon yell, "Dave!" I turned around and ran back with gun drawn, expecting to see him on the ground with the three prisoners wrestling for his gun. When I came around the corner, he was standing with two of our prisoners. The third one was gone. Leon said he ran off into the brush. He didn't dare leave the other two. We took them to the truck and were sure we would be able to catch the third one. We radioed for more troops and dogs. There was a fairly intense search, but we didn't find him. That's the way life is. Some days you're the windshield, some days you're the bug!

About two months later, an Anchorage resident found my handcuffs in his yard and turned them in to the Anchorage Police Department. My social security number was engraved on them so they contacted me and returned them. They had been cut off with bolt cutters. That suspect became known as "the one that got away".

*****

One fall just before hunting season when hunters were target shooting and preparing for the upcoming moose season, I received a call about a moose poaching. The location was behind a gravel pit on the Knik River, which was being used as a shooting range.

I located the moose remains and found that someone had shot it from the range. The two hindquarters had been removed and the rest left to rot. Waste of big game meat is one of the most disgusting violations and it makes all of the legal hunters angry, as well as the people who just like to see game around. The Alaska courts are severe on violators who leave meat to rot.

It pays to check closely all around the area where a poaching took place. We have identified and successfully prosecuted poachers who have dropped a variety of items at the scene. Among those things found were hunting knives with initials on them, driver licenses, hunting licenses and whole wallets.

One individual illegally took a moose, loaded it into his pickup, turned around in the road and headed for home. He would have gotten away with it except that, while turning around in the road, he had backed into the snow berm. As

117

he drove off, he left one thing behind... the clear impression of his license plate and number in the snow berm.

In the case of the shooting range poaching, I eventually found a nametag, which displayed the name "Bill". The color and the design of the nametag looked familiar. I recognized it as being from Stuart Andersons Cattle Company restaurant in Anchorage.

Upon reaching the restaurant I contacted the manager. It turned out that there were two "Bills" who worked there. After interviewing both of them, it became obvious which one was my suspect. I concentrated on him and he soon admitted that he had been there at the moose kill. A friend of his had shot the moose and, along with another friend, took the hindquarters. They told Bill that, if he wanted some moose meat, he could go get the rest of it. Bill went, but he decided not to take any meat. He then gave me the names of his friends.

I contacted the two poachers at their residences and obtained confessions from them. They took me to the moose meat in the freezer.

Both men had large, expensive homes and worked at the local federal post office making large salaries. They could both easily afford to buy meat without poaching. There was definitely no excuse for not taking all the meat after they did poach it. The icing on the cake was that the one man already had a large chest-freezer full of moose meat. It was from the previous year. They very seldom ate moose meat

Linda had an artist neighbor build this salmon plaque for me. It included built-on mounts for the recovered handcuffs. (Photo by Linda Carpenter)

because he was the only person in the family that liked it.

*****

The Palmer patrol area contained both grizzly bears and brown bears. Basically they are the same species of bear. If they are found within fifty miles of salt water, they are considered brown bears. If they are inland over fifty miles from salt water, they are considered to be grizzlies. The term "Grizzly" actually comes from the white hairs found in their brown coat giving them a grizzled look. On some grizzlies, the white hairs are very prominent and those bears are referred to as "silver tips".

There are three adjoining lakes, which are connected by a channel of water north of Palmer (Lakes Louise, Susitna and Tyone). There is an over abundance of grizzly bears in that area. Since there is also a large number of remote cabins on those lakes, the bears have been a serious problem for many years. They seem to know when nobody is around and they like to pretend they're a D-9 Cat and destroy cabins.

I have known cabin owners to nail spiked boards on their steps and porches. Some board up the doors and windows with spiked boards when they leave. Some have set booby traps for the bears. Nothing seems to work. The bears still get in. One guy wrapped bacon slices around a can of Raid. From the looks of the cabin afterward, the bear bit into the Raid can, went into a bit of a snit and demolished the interior of the cabin.

Some cabin owners want to kill every bear they see and it's hard to blame them.

*****

120

I received a radio dispatch one day to meet a Fort Richardson soldier down at Goose Bay. He had shot a brown bear in self-defense while hunting moose and it had gotten away. I contacted him and he took me to the area where he had shot the bear. It was a very brushy area and the bear had run off into the thick of it.

We did not want a wounded bear in the area. Our only choice was to make sure it was dead or finish it off. It was very unnerving to be searching for the wounded animal in the dark trees and brush. I had the twelve-gauge pump loaded with slugs and buckshot and was glad to have it.

The soldier was tight behind me with his moose rifle. I appreciated having him along. A lot of men would have not wanted to take part in the search.

We located the dead bear lying behind a log. I don't know if he just died there or if he was laying in wait for his pursuers when he finally died. It could have happened either way.

*****

There was a big game guide in the Talkeetna Mountains about sixty miles north of Palmer who knew the country better than anyone else and became a living legend of Alaska. He took his hunters in on horseback and always gave them a good hunt.

He reportedly kept canned food cached in various areas of the mountains and used it for their meals during the hunts. After a period of time, the labels all came off the cans leaving the contents anonymous. If there were four people in his party, he would dig out eight cans and empty the contents into a kettle and heat it over the fire. I guess sometimes this "Surprise stew" would turn out good and other times… well, imagine peaches or pears in your stew.

This guide tried to run an honest hunt and keep his hunters legal. He got very upset with one particular group who wouldn't listen to him and shot an illegal animal. The guide brought a videotape of the hunters in to our office and reported the violation.

The most incredible part of the videotape was where the guide, himself, performed a feat of which most men would be incapable. He pulled a long hair from a horse's tail, made a loop in it and laid on the creek bank dangling the horse hair in the water. Eventually he gave a jerk of the wrist and flipped a grayling up on the bank. He had floated the loop over the fish and snared it!

*****

I had several gold claims in the same area of the Talkeetna Mountains and had built a short airstrip on one. One day my brother, Greg, and I flew in and landed on a claim above mine, near the mountaintop.

This claim belonged to some other miners I knew. As we exited the plane and walked toward the tent camp, we saw a young bull moose watching us. As we got closer, he ran over to us, making us feel uneasy. We knew how dangerous moose can be. We walked around a bulldozer, and the moose followed us. We continued walking toward the tents. He followed behind, at times with his head over our shoulder. There was no one in camp. We entered the cook tent to evade the moose. He wandered off, but not very far.

Our walk back to the plane was uneventful. We later learned that the moose was a camp pet and was probably looking for a handout. I wish we had known that at the time.

I probably wouldn't have those six gray hairs that Linda claims I have.

*****

At the Palmer post I enjoyed working with one of the most dedicated and talented Wildlife Troopers in the Department. Garland had been a decorated helicopter pilot during the Vietnam War. He was also an excellent fixed-wing and helicopter pilot for the Public Safety Department.

Garland and I had many interesting experiences and trips together over the years. But he had his share of close calls too. The one in particular that comes to mind is almost unbelievable.

Garland was working with the Super Cub on the Alaska Peninsula. Roy, another Wildlife Trooper was working with him. It seems to me that they were operating out of the Sandy River cabin, which I described in a previous story. They had the Super Cub tied down and were waiting out a windstorm. After the storm, Garland and Roy did a thorough pre-flight inspection of the Cub and paid special attention to the wing struts and attachments. Everything checked out okay.

They took off from the strip by the cabin and gained an altitude of about one hundred feet before a strut broke loose from the wing. The plane immediately dropped out of the air and landed upside down in the river. Garland was underwater and dazed. Roy, who was in the back seat, had his head above water, but his foot was trapped underneath the front seat. He was able to reach Garland and hold his head above water until he came to. Garland then managed to free Roy's foot from the seat. They helped each other through the shallow water to shore. Garland remembered the survival kit in the Cub and went back to retrieve it.

Roy was injured and was not able to hike the distance back to the Sandy River cabin. Luckily there was another cabin close by. They made it to that cabin where they found two old sleeping bags. Being wet and cold, they lay in the sleeping bags shivering and trying to warm up.

A local guide flew by and spotted the airplane in the river. He landed and found Garland and Roy. He transported them to the nearest medical attention. Garland was okay, but Roy suffered an injured hip in the crash. He was laid up in the hospital for a short period of time, but he healed fast and was soon back to work.

Garland had been a close friend of ours for several years and we were shaken by the news of his close call. We were very grateful that he and Roy survived.

*****

Working in Alaska for the Department of Public Safety had its fun times, but there were time that weren't so enjoyable. One of those times occurred in the fall of 1983 when some moose hunters found a human body, which had been buried in a gravel bar of the Knik River. A second body was located shortly afterward. They were the bodies of strip club dancers out of Anchorage.

Dancers had been regularly coming up missing for about three years. Of course, it was not all that unusual for the dancers to pack up and leave without notifying their employers, but some of the girls were missing under suspicious circumstances. The two bodies found were identified as missing dancers and it was then known that there was a serial killer loose in the area.

The blue shirt troopers and the brown shirt troopers worked together in some of the search duties. We dug sand and gravel and filtered it through a screen to find any possible evidence that may have been left at those areas. It was not fun. It was gruesome work.

The blue shirt investigators did a fantastic job of working the case and, after a long, hard pull, caught the perpetrator. He confessed to many slayings of strip club dancers. In all, he was responsible for the rapes and killings of twenty-five to thirty girls. Approximately half of the bodies were recovered. He was a well respected businessman who owned a bakery.

A book entitled "Butcher Baker" has been written which describes the investigation in detail.

*****

In 1980, I was assigned to work the Alaska Peninsula during the brown bear season. I secreted my camouflaged tent in the alders and found a good spot in the trees from which to watch for planes coming into and leaving this area. There were a lot of bears there and we expected there might be some illegal guiding practices.

After some long days, I would curl up in a cozy sleeping bag and read by lantern. As always, I would hear strange noises outside the tent. I had made camp next to a beautiful stream, which provided my water and helped put me to sleep at night.

One night in particular, the stream was noisier than usual. I heard animals wading through the water. I heard that every night, but this night was different. It "really" sounded like animals wading. I opened the front flap of the tent and stuck my head out. It was pretty dark, but there was enough light for me to see a herd of caribou wading up the creek to about fifty feet from the tent and then up on the bank on the other side.

Later that night, after thinking about all the sights and sounds I had been seeing and hearing, I was inspired to write an article. The article was sincere and the words came easily. Here is that article I wrote late one night in 1980:

## Who is the Real Lord of the Bush?
### by Dave Carpenter

Having been with the Alaska Department of Public Safety for seven years, the past five as a Fish and Wildlife Protection Officer, I have had the opportunity of observing hundreds of outdoorsmen in the field. These outdoorsmen range from resident Alaskans to visitors from the lower forty-nine states and even a wide variety from foreign countries. Their activities include everything from sport fishing to bear hunting.

One thing I have found to be in common with nearly all hunters and outdoorsmen is the irony between how man sees himself in the wilderness and how he really fits in. I believe that once a man realizes the difference between his perception of himself and the reality of his position, he may be able to improve upon his outdoor abilities and become more in tune with nature.

The creatures of the wild were considered to be the masters of the wilderness many years ago before the invention of a long, narrow tool made of hard wood and cold steel, which was capable of moving a projectile through the air at a tremendously high velocity. Certainly, man was no match for the strength of the big bear. The big bear was the undisputed king of the bush. Now, with the high-powered rifle in his hand, man tends to feel that he is the master of the wilderness, second to none. After having spent considerable time in the bush areas of Alaska, and having met and visited with a large number of bear hunters in the state, my view of this theory is somewhat different.

Man is the ruler in the bush today. No creature, large or small, can stand up to the viciousness of the big gun. Man is superior. Man is brave. Man is the most fearsome animal in the bush, but only during the daylight hours! What man can see, he does not fear...as long as he holds in his hands the big gun much as a babe holds onto his security blanket.

Oh, what a difference during the hours of darkness! Man stumbles and fumbles around in the night. Man does fear what he cannot see and, unfortunately, once darkness falls, man sees nothing and fears everything. Man depends solely upon his eyes for "seeing". He cannot use his underdeveloped sense of smell to "see" whether or not there are animals in the area. His hearing is not acute enough to "see" that what he's hearing may be only a ground squirrel scurrying through the grass. As daylight wanes and nighttime falls, man becomes a helpless creature... the most helpless creature in the bush! Huddled in his two-man tent, he hears all kinds of strange noises. He is completely out of his element. The mighty hunter begins to feel that maybe he is now the hunted. A ptarmigan flushes and startles him... fearsome birds, they. Raindrops pattering on the leaves may sound like footfalls of an unknown beast. The wind, with its myriad pitches and swishes, becomes an ominous sound. The stream, which runs directly in front of the tent, indeed, at night changes from what was a pleasant babble to a cacophony of dangerous and devious night sounds; sounds of objects dropping, of footfalls and of large animals wading across the creek... always toward the one whose imagination is working overtime. The hunter is in the bear's domain, not they in his. He sleeps with the bears, not they with him.

But, at last another sleepless night has ended. The darkness has left and the light of day has arrived. Now he can get up and out of his tent and (with his rifle close by always) travel through the wilderness country, again the mighty, fearless "Lord of the bush".

Having a large caliber weapon in his possession does not make a man the master of his environment, nor even a good woodsman. Most hunters and outdoorsmen, myself included, use only a very small fraction of their abilities to sense what is going on around them. A great deal could be done to improve upon this deficiency.

I would encourage anyone who wants to spend time in the wilderness to make more efficient use of his outdoor time by paying more attention to detail. He could make an effort to be more observant of his surroundings. Through patience and diligence, he can locate the source of the sound he is hearing and become familiar with it. When he hears that same sound at night, instead of fear, there will be knowledge. He will become more a part of his environment. Practically everything of nature has an odor. Some odors are stronger than others, but it is always there. When a man observes an odor strange to him he could again trace it to its source and identify it. It may turn out to be plants, stagnant water or a bull elk in the rut. Once the odor is learned, it will not be a mystery when encountered in the dark. Only when man can distinguish the sounds and smells of nature, can he consider himself to be in touch with nature.

*****

Once an outdoorsman has had the experience of being at home in the wilderness, enjoying the sounds and smells as well as the sights of the bush, he can use his mind and imagination to lead to a creative portion of his life... after all, that's how this article was written... on the bank of a clear stream in my two-man tent on the Alaska Peninsula. The next morning became a warm sunny day following a long, windy and rainy night interspersed with a wide variety of night sounds. I realized then that I was just beginning to "see" nature.

*****

I received a call one day about a moose that had stepped into a wolf trap and was limping around with the trap still attached to his leg a few inches above his hoof. The moose was reported to be up the Knik River halfway to the Knik Glacier. I went to Fish and Game to get a biologist and a tranquilizer gun. There was only one biologist in the office and he could not leave. He made up two tranquilizer darts for me. We could only guess at the amount of tranquilizer to use so we guessed on the light side to make sure we didn't overdose the bull.

I drove my four wheel drive Blazer up the Knik River Road and down onto the gravel bars of the river. There are several miles of road along the gravel bars heading up toward the Knik Glacier. I located the moose with the wolf trap still on his leg. He was a beautiful big bull with a nice set of antlers. I was able to walk up to within forty feet of him. He just stood and watched me. This was going to be easy. I fired the dart directly into his hindquarter. In a few minutes he would lie down and I would be able to remove the trap. Except he didn't, so I couldn't.

129

He apparently didn't like the feeling of the tranquilizer working, because he started kicking. I've seen horses and mules kick, but that's the first time I had seen a moose kick. Their hind legs are very powerful. His kicks had a long reach and were lightning fast. I decided right then that I'd rather be kicked by a horse or mule. I understood then how a moose could kill a wolf that was attacking it, with those swift kicks and those sharp hooves.

The moose then took off running. He was supposed to go down, but he was running into the trees and up the hillside! I watched and waited, not wanting to chase him farther up the hill. Finally, he went down. I climbed up to him, but was concerned about grabbing onto his hind leg to remove the trap. He was looking around, but appeared immobilized. When he looked away and rested his chin on the ground, I very cautiously removed the trap. It had cut into his leg, but there were no broken bones. I didn't have any antidote to give him, so I backed off and waited around until he finally got back up and, after a few minutes, wobbled off. I knew then that he would be okay.

*****

In the winter of 1987, I was called out to Matanuska Lake where a moose had fallen through the ice and was unable to get back up onto it. When I arrived, I found that it was a cow moose, which appeared to be in good condition, and she was about forty feet from shore. The ice was too thick for her to break with her front hooves.

A friend of ours lived on the lake just a few hundred yards away. I borrowed a canoe from him and took the axe out of my patrol vehicle. After chopping a hole through the ice near shore large enough to get the canoe into the water, I was able to work my way toward the moose. It was a matter of chopping about a foot or two of ice in front of the canoe, then paddling forward to reach the solid ice and chopping again.

I suppose it took about half an hour to reach the hole where the moose had fallen through. I wasn't really sure how she would react if I were to chop through that final couple of feet of ice with her facing me. Would she recognize it as an escape route and be desperate enough to make a beeline for the channel I had just chopped for her, even though it meant going over the top of me to do it? If she did that, would I just be brushed aside or cut up by those sharp hooves? My friend on the shore shouted words of encouragement. Sure, he was feeling mighty brave. I admit, I did feel better knowing he was there. At least he could show the divers the approximate location of my body.

It actually turned out better than I had expected. The moose turned away and was trying to go the other direction, probably thinking my intentions were not in her best interest. That gave me a chance to break through the last piece of ice separating her from the shore. I paddled back through the channel to the shore and we dragged the canoe out of the way.

I thought I might have to approach her from the other side to get her started toward the channel, but it wasn't necessary. It didn't take her long to figure out where to go. My friend and I were both relieved when she made it onto shore, walked a few feet away and began eating brush as though nothing had happened.

*****

During my twenty years with the Department of Public Safety, I spent a lot of time in the bush. I always felt comfortable and well prepared for any situation that might come up in the outdoors. A large portion of my training and preparedness I owe to a good friend of mine, John Nicholson.

Linda and I met John and his wife, Donna, back in 1971 and immediately became close friends. John and I spent a lot time together over the years and have shared a lot of wonderful hunting and fishing trips.

I remember one moose hunt John and I went on with a canoe on the Tyone River. We usually planned on taking just one moose as that provided enough meat for both families along with our caribou. It was a long, exhausting day getting our canoe near the area we wanted to hunt. We had spent the entire day at last minute packing, driving to our launch area and canoeing to a cabin which used to belong to a friend of mine and now belongs to the State. It was available to anyone who needed it. That night, we needed it.

We secured our canoe and hauled our sleeping bags and rifles inside. The cabin was very basic and quite rustic. We leaned our rifles against the wall, threw our sleeping bags on the bunks and hit the sack. Before long, we heard the padding of soft, heavy footfalls on the front porch. The first thought that came to my mind was that it was a grizzly bear. That whole area was loaded with grizzlies. The door was not latched. In fact, there was no latch. The door was just there... free to swing open or closed with the breeze. We hadn't worried about it and made no effort to block it closed. And now there was something on the front porch, possibly a bear.

John whispered across the room from his bunk to mine, "It's either a bear or a porcupine."

A porcupine never occurred to me. It sounded too heavy for anything smaller than a bear. I quietly slipped across the room and grabbed our rifles. We had nothing to prop against the door. We could only wait at our bunks and listen. John moved to the window and looked out. It <u>was</u> a porcupine. I looked out and couldn't believe it. He had sure fooled me.

I would like to say here that I never used anyone's cabin out in the bush without leaving a note with my name, phone number and the date I was there. I usually mentioned the condition of the cabin and any damage that appeared to have been recently done. If the door had been kicked in or a window broken out, it would be left on the note. I would not use any fuel or food stores except in an emergency. In that case, I would ask on the note for them to contact me so I could replace what I used and thank them personally. If you use their kindling and firewood to warm up, you must chop more. The next person may need it more than you did. An owner may only get to his cabin once every month or two, but they generally appreciate having others treat their place with respect.

The next day we got up and continued into our hunting area. It was the day before the opening of moose season. We set up camp and did some scouting around before dark. I remember both of us lying down on our bellies on a grassy ledge watching a young bull moose feeding directly below us. He never knew how lucky he was that the season didn't open for several more hours.

The next morning, we hunted that same general area. John had spotted a giant bull caribou across the river and we watched him for a while. He was very large with a possible record-book set of antlers and a big white cape. He was also very lucky; we were hunting moose, not caribou. A short time later, three trophy-sized caribou trotted past me without ever realizing I was there. Any one of the three would have made a very respectable mount.

Later that day, John and I were about a hundred feet apart and out of each other's sight when we both spotted a young bull moose on the riverbank. We took him. We quartered him up and loaded him into the canoe. We laid the meat, in meat sacks, on top of sticks in the bottom of the canoe to keep it dry. We loaded our gear on top. We then headed out of the area and back toward home.

That night we set up camp on the riverbank. We hung the moose meat from a tree branch a short distance above our camp and tied a tarp above it for weather protection. We entered our tent and crawled into our sleeping bags. They provided a welcome warmth from the cold night air. Things couldn't have been more perfect.

A few hours later, John was awakened by a low growling noise. He recognized it as a bear growl. He opened the tent flap and peered out. There, on top of the river bank, silhouetted against the dark evening sky, was our hanging moose meat and a very large bear leaning into the meat and sniffing it! No—-wait a minute. He heard the growling sound again, but it was coming from behind him. He turned and then realized the noise was me snoring and doing a pretty fair impression of a bear's growl.

He woke me up and when I looked out toward the moose meat, I could see that the dark outline John had seen was the tarp over the meat. The way we had tied it off made it resemble a big bear on all fours with his neck outstretched toward our moose meat. The remainder of the night was more restful.

We made it out the next day and all the way home with no major mishaps. We have never had a bad moose (referring to the quality of the meat) and that one was as good as any we'd ever had.

In addition to being the best outdoorsman I have ever seen, John Nicholson is also one of the best hunters and fishermen in the state of Alaska. My time spent with John and the knowledge of the Alaskan outdoors I gained from him has been invaluable.

John and Donna still live in Anchorage and operate "Rainbow Expeditions". John guides sport fishermen from all over the world to the very best fishing in the state and his fishermen are regularly breaking world records.

*****

# HAINES TOUR

During our last few years at Palmer, we kept hearing good things about Haines in Southeast Alaska. It seemed that nearly everyone who had been stationed in Haines at one time or another wanted to retire there eventually. We decided we wanted to experience Southeast and Haines might be a good place to start. In the summer of 1988 the Haines post came open. We put in for it and got it.

I made a trip to Haines to check on housing. We ended up buying a beautiful home with complete privacy overlooking the mountains and the Lynn Canal. The Lynn Canal is one of the most picturesque parts of the Pacific Ocean. It is also one of the longest and deepest fjords on the North American continent.

The mountains on both sides of the canal are not smooth half-hearted mountains. They are rugged and real. The most impressive portion of these Chilkat Mountains are the Cathedral Peaks. They are well known and easily visible from town.

Historic Ft. Seward is located on the very edge of town and is one of Haines' main attractions. The group of large, beautiful two-story houses were once an active army base. The army shut it down after World War II and it was purchased by civilians. Those beautiful buildings are now residences, shops, restaurants, etc. Ft. Seward is the location of the Chilkat Tglingit dancers, the Lynn Canal Community Players and a terrific outdoor salmon bake at the tribal house.

The Haines area has two great lakes for recreation. Chilkoot Lake can be easily reached by vehicle and Chilkat Lake can be reached by riverboat or, in the winter, by snow machine.

The two state parks, Chilkoot Park and Chilkat Park are very popular with people and brown bears.

The road north goes past the Tglingit village of Klukwan and forty miles from Haines is Pleasant Camp. Pleasant Camp is the U.S./Canada border where you enter British Columbia. It is about 750 miles from Haines, through British Columbia and Yukon Territory, to Anchorage. Some of the road was very rough, usually making it an overnight trip, but occasionally we made it in one day.

\*\*\*\*\*

The Haines trooper post was located in a second story building above the grocery store. It had two rooms. The small front room housed the Department of Motor Vehicles, which was run by a very knowledgeable and helpful individual, Elaine Piggot. Those of us who worked with her became very fond and appreciative of Elaine.

The larger back room served as the office for the blue shirt trooper and myself. There was one blue shirt and one brown shirt in Haines. That was it! There were times when we could have used more.

During the four years I worked in Haines, I worked with two different blue shirts. I was lucky. They were both exceptional. They were both good at their job and well liked by the community. Quentin was tall, handsome and gentlemanly. When Quentin transferred out later on, Don transferred in. Don was a 300-pound mountain of a man with a black belt in Karate. I enjoyed working with both of them.

At the Haines post I was well equipped. I had a twenty-nine foot salt-water patrol boat, a riverboat, a canoe, a snow machine and a four-wheel-drive pickup. I needed it all to patrol the salt water, the rivers, the lakes and the backcountry.

I enjoyed going up to Pleasant Camp and tried to do it routinely once every week or two. I would patrol my way up, visit the U.S. border guards and then with the Canadian guards. They were all good people and were very helpful to us.

Occasionally Haines had a serious bear problem. They would come into town and cause a ruckus. The worst time of the year was in the fall when several of the locals fired up their smokers in their wooded back yards and were smoking salmon. The bears could smell the smoke houses from a long ways away and couldn't resist trying to get into them. During that time, people/bear confrontations were a very real danger.

*****

Probably the most valuable pieces of art in Alaska are the Chilkat blankets which are woven by the Chilkat Tlingit Indians. They are actually more of a shawl than a blanket and are worn during ceremonial dances. They were not designed to be used for warmth.

The blankets were woven with the hair of the mountain goats, which are prevalent in the mountainous Haines area. The blankets are totally hand woven. It can take up to a year to produce one of the Chilkat blankets and they are worth thousands of dollars. Unfortunately, the skills required to produce a Chilkat blanket, along with many other traditional skills, are being lost. The young people today don't appear to have enough interest to learn the skills.

Haines has a wonderful museum in the center of town. The Sheldon Museum has lots of information about the blankets and their production. A visit to Haines would not be complete without time spent at the Sheldon Museum.

Another traditional skill, which can still be appreciated in all of Southeast, is the carving of totem poles. Haines does not have as many poles as some of the other southeast communities, but it does have a fair number. Unlike the Chilkat blankets, totem poles seem to have plenty of active producers.

*****

There is an area a few miles south of Haines at the base of Davidson Glacier called Glacier Point. It's a large grassy area with a glacial lake and many small potholes of water. There are no people living there. Occasionally, while

139

boating by or flying over the area, we would see a white horse moving about munching grass. He had been left there years earlier. A white horse in an area populated by brown bears! How did he survive the bears all those years and the winters where several feet of snow is the norm? Whatever the answers are, we know he had to be one tough horse.

*****

During my first winter in Haines, I received a call from a man saying he had been seeing a moose around for the last couple of days and he had just now heard a gunshot. I went to the area and searched the woods. I found a freshly killed pregnant cow moose. There were small patches of snow on the ground and I found a few boot prints nearby. I drew a sketch of the boot print and set about to contact the local residents. As I talked to them, I had them come outside so I could describe to them where the dead moose was. That gave me a chance to see their boot prints. At the third house, I found my man. He eventually admitted to the poaching.

The cow had been pregnant with twin calves so he had actually killed three moose. The townspeople were so angry with him that, after he was fined in court, they literally gave him such a bad time he had to leave town.

*****

During my four years in Haines, I had two cow moose incidents that turned out to be quite unusual. One incident was when a hunter shot a bull moose and the bullet passed completely through the body of the bull and struck the cow moose behind him.

140

The other incident was when a hunter shot at a bull and the cow moose, standing slightly behind the bull, stepped forward and caught the bullet. That story was confirmed by the hoof prints in the snow.

In both cases, the hunters reported the incidents them selves and were not charged with violations. The meat, of course, was donated to charity.

*****

When we were preparing for the move to Haines, part of the lure was the hunting down there. I knew there was a moose season and I knew there were deer in the area. So I assumed the hunting would be good.

I was disappointed to learn that moose hunting was a one day thing. Fish and Game flew over the valley and, when they counted about seventeen moose down, blew a siren from the aircraft. They'd fly up and down the valley and over town blowing that weird siren. The intent was to avoid going over their limit of twenty moose taken. My first year in Haines, the season lasted for four hours and was over by noon.

As it turned out there were a few deer in the area, but not enough for a hunting season without going south toward Juneau.

There was a mountain goat season and a brown bear season which I enjoyed working. I was not interested in hunting either species, as I am a meat hunter.

*****

Haines was lucky enough to have the best state park ranger I have ever met. His name is Bill Zack, but he goes by the name "Zack". He's a hard worker and very knowledgeable.

Zack had a close call with a brown bear before I got there. He had reports of an aggressive bear in the park and went out there with the blue shirt trooper to check it out. As he was tacking up the "Beware of bear" sign, the bear came after him. Zack very coolly emptied his .357 caliber handgun into the bear and was lucky to have Quentin there with the shotgun to finish it off. The bear died at Zack's feet.

I worked with Zack on a few occasions and helped him capture and transport a wounded eagle. The eagle was shipped to the Sitka rehabilitation center where it would be doctored back to health and released back into the wild. Capturing eagles can be a dangerous activity. Their talons and beaks are formidable weapons.

The eagles in the Haines area on the Chilkat River are an attraction to tourists and photographers from around the world. Because of warm springs upriver at the confluence of the Chilkat and Tsirku Rivers, a section of the river stays open all winter. All other rivers freeze up. This leaves the spawning chum salmon available to the eagles for food. Eagles come from other areas to a four or five mile stretch of the river and number up to 3,500 some winters.

With that many eagles in such a short stretch, the photographic opportunities are endless. Since so many eagles gather there, the area has become known as the "Council Grounds". The Haines Highway runs parallel with the Chilkat River and makes the area very accessible.

Woody Bausch, a good friend of ours in Haines who happened to be a professional photographer, spent countless

Eagle tree on Chilkat River. (Photo by author)

hours photographing the Chilkat eagles. Some of his photos have appeared in magazines, and some are now highly admired postcards available in gifts shops throughout Southeast Alaska.

*****

My patrol boat was a twenty-nine foot gillnetter with a 200 horsepower outboard on the stern. It had a cabin with a cookstove and two bunks. I had the department put in radar for night patrols.

Some of my patrols were conducted alone and some were with my summer aide. Boarding fishing boats in rough water was a challenge when I was by myself. I had to maneuver up against the other boat, exit the cabin, go out onto the deck, grab the tie-up line and get onto the fishing boat before it drifted or was blown away by the winds.

On dry, starlit nights I would occasionally sleep on the deck of the boat and I have many fond memories of those nights. I would turn our eight-foot rubber boat upside-down and use it like a giant air mattress. I would lay in my sleeping bag on deck and let the gentle waves rock me to sleep. On darks nights, I could look and watch the sky come to life with falling stars, constellations and satellites regularly going overhead.

Usually, during a fishery, I would sleep for a couple of hours and go back on patrol for a while. Then, I would anchor up out of sight of the fishing boats and sleep for a couple more hours before going back out. Anything to keep them guessing where I was.

*****

Haines is a gold mine for strange people, like me, who for some perverse reason like to cut, split and stack firewood. We've always had fireplaces and wood stoves and I have always enjoyed working with the wood. Short distances out of Haines, there are logging roads that go back into areas of abundant firewood. With the type of winters we had in Haines, we needed to stockpile a lot of wood. There was also a continuous supply of logs washing up on the beach. We had wide tires on our truck and could drive down the beach and back up to the logs. We got a lot of great wood that way.

*****

Skagway is just a half hour by boat from Haines up Taiya Inlet. The population of Skagway was 700 as compared to 1,800 in Haines. There was a city police department there, but we had jurisdiction over anything that occurred outside the city limits.

Skagway is a fun town to visit. There is a lot of history there and it looks much like it did during the gold rush of 1898. The stores and hotels are old-timey, kept in good condition and painted beautifully. There is an old-fashioned ice cream parlor, which gets very busy on hot summer days when the cruise ships are in. The Fourth of July is always fun in Skagway.

The grave of Skagway's famous outlaw, Soapy Smith, is located just a few miles out of town in the Gold Rush Cemetery. About nine miles out of Skagway at Dyea is the start of the historic Chilkoot Trail. This trail is a thirty-three mile hike through rugged country, which had been negotiated by all those gold prospectors back in 1898. They, of course, were required to pack along a year's supply of food, which amounted to about 1,150 pounds and thirty trips. Many of the objects that the thousands of prospectors left behind along the trail are still there to see. Hikers are not allowed to take them.

On two different occasions, I stood at the start of the forty-five degree climb and imagined what it must have been like back in those days. Linda and I talked several times about how we should load up our backpacks and make that hike while we were living so close. It would have taken four or five days. Unfortunately we never found the time to do it.

*****

Juneau headquarters sent me a summer aide to help work the commercial fishery along with the sport fishery. He was a middle-aged German man, Herb, who stayed in a camp trailer in our backyard. He came with his faithful sidekick, Troll. Troll was a rottweiller and the best trained dog we had ever seen. Linda and I became very attached to him.

Troll was a people-friendly dog and soon became known and well liked around town. Herb never went anywhere without him. We took Troll out with us on the patrol boat until some fishermen complained about being intimidated by him and the department asked us to leave him home from then on. That was a sad day for both Herb and Troll. Linda had to "Troll-sit" after that when Herb and I were gone on the fisheries.

It was comical at the end of the season when people would come up to me and say something like, "Where's Troll and the other guy?" Nobody seemed to remember Herb's name, but they all remembered Troll's.

Leaving Haines harbor on "Challenger" for commercial
fishery patrol. Author and Troll on deck.
(Photo by Linda Carpenter)

The great thing about working on the salt water of Alaska is that you get to see a lot of animals. We were continually seeing whales, seals, killer whales, sea birds, etc.

On one patrol out of Juneau, I was working with our Hoonah trooper in a Boston Whaler. Somewhere in the same area was our sixty-foot patrol vessel the "Enforcer".

The Whaler is just an open skiff, which allows you to feel the spindrift coming off the waves and hear the sounds of the ocean in addition to providing much better visibility in all directions than a closed cabin.

Howard and I were approaching a bay when we saw some movement a short distance away. It looked like whales jumping. We motored over that direction and soon realized that it was a pod of approximately twenty killer whales jumping completely out of the water and landing with a big splash.

Killer whales get up to thirty feet long and have a very tall dorsal fin. They are black and white and beautiful. They were jumping and diving, jumping and diving and coming our direction. We shut off our engine and waited, hoping one wouldn't jump and land on our boat. They went by us on both sides of the boat. The ones that were directly in line with us landed just before our boat and came up on the other side just past us. It was one of the most incredible sights I have ever seen. I only wish we had had a video camera ready. The whales had to have seen the skiff and were careful to avoid colliding with it.

We had real winters in Haines. With the moisture that is provided to a seacoast area plus the cold weather of the interior, we got a sizable amount of snow. In fact, we got twenty feet of snow one winter.

We were having our pickup and the state pickup plowed out whenever we got a deep snow. Finally we gave up on our personal truck and just had the state truck plowed out. Our truck then became completely buried and was just a bump in the snow out in the yard. I spent most of my spare time each day shoveling. We had to shovel off the roof of the house twice. Our property looked like a rat maze with deep trenches going to the truck, the woodpile, and other areas. I had to build a special A-frame to keep the snow from crushing our boat.

The deep snow kept vehicles limited to the main roads as the back roads were plugged. That's when the snow machines came out. The Haines area is beautiful snow machine country and patrolling by snow machine was actually very enjoyable.

The blue shirt and I sometimes teamed up and ran our snow machine patrols together. We would patrol back to the ghost town of Porcupine, which used to be a bustling gold rush community. We would patrol to the top of Flour Mountain and over to Chilkat Lake where several of the local residents had weekend cabins. Fortunately, these patrols turned out to be essentially uneventful without any poachings found and no search and rescues necessary.

*****

While working out of Haines, I was able to spend a lot of time in Sitka for training classes at the academy and for the herring fishery, which took place each spring.

Some of the additional training classes they sent us back to the academy for were physical fitness, navigation, firearms proficiency, self-defense (where we took turns beating each other up) and the use of "Capstun".

Capstun is a highly effective pepper spray to be used for self-defense during aggravated confrontations. I think Capstun was a great addition to our arsenal. It's a good tool that fills the wide gap between having to roll around in the mud with criminals or having to shoot them. With Capstun you can bring things under control and not have to injure anyone. The spray stings the eyes so they can't be opened and makes the recipient so miserable that it takes the fight out of him. In about forty-five minutes the effects are gone and he's as good as new.

The problem was that those in charge of running our department had a perverse sense of humor. They felt that, if we were going to use Capstun on someone, we should know what it feels like to be doused with it. I wasn't convinced.

They sent us down to the academy where we had classes on the effects of Capstun, what it is comprised of and how it works. We then gathered outside where, one at a time, we had to walk up face to face with one of the academy staff and let him hit us in the face with the pepper spray. It was quite exhilarating! Our eyes instantly snapped shut and we were helpless. A few of the guys went down on their knees. I think a small dab of Capstun on a moose hindquarter would deter a hungry wolverine.

We were then guided into the showers where we shampooed and scrubbed hoping that it would eliminate the sting. It didn't. It still took forty-five minutes before we felt normal.

Later that night, down at the local pub, one of our guys, who hadn't shampooed thoroughly enough, had some sweat run down his forehead and into his eyes and went through the pain all over again.

*****

Each spring found us in Sitka to work the highly unpredictable herring fishery. The town loads up with fishermen, Fish and Game biologists, and Fish and Wildlife Troopers. Every day the biologists take samples of herring, test the roe in an attempt to catch it in its prime state and report the results to the fishermen during the daily morning meeting. This can go on for a couple of weeks until the herring roe appears to be perfect. At that time the biologists will announce the opening of the fishery. The duration of the fishery tends to be short-lived and can be as short as half an hour.

As short as the fishery is, there is a lot of money to be made. A boat in the right location can haul in full nets of herring and end up with a full boat of fish. This short fishery can provide an entire year's wages for a skipper and his crew.

Our job as Fish and Wildlife Protection Troopers was to be out in the middle of the fishery in our patrol boats watching for violations and refereeing confrontations between fishermen. The most common violations were fishing too early or fishing too late. A few minutes before the opening, Fish and Game would do a countdown over the marine radio. They would count down to the last second and then announce the opening. If a boat launched its seine (net) ten or fifteen seconds too early, it could scoop up all the fish that several boats would normally be sharing. That boat's skipper would have to release all his fish, be summoned to court and fined. It was important to not allow early fishing.

Fishing after the closure could not be allowed either. An additional minute or two of fishing could bring in an extra 10,000 to 20,000 dollars. The only way to prevent boats from doing it is to be strict on the closure times.

Sitka is a picturesque town with a lot of history and was the state capital of Alaska from 1884-1900. The capital was then moved to Juneau where it still is today. Just being in Sitka during the herring fishery was exciting to those of us who enjoy and appreciate Alaskan history.

*****

Whenever the blue shirt left Haines I would cover for him and handle his emergencies. He did the same for me. I don't know how he did it, but he seemed to know exactly when to leave town. The rest of us in town got nervous when he left, because we knew something bad was going to happen.

With the blue shirt out of town I handled calls ranging from theft, burglaries, assaults, suicides and even a wildman from Juneau who was threatening lives and mentally disturbed enough to carry out his threats. I ended up arresting him and transporting him to Juneau for psychiatric care. Over a year later, while stationed in Anchorage, I received paperwork in the form of a million dollar lawsuit from that individual for false arrest. Fortunately, the courts did not accept the lawsuit and it never went anywhere.

Hollywood came to Haines in 1991. The cast and crew arrived to Film "White Fang". What a culture shock it was for them to come from California where they could get anything they wanted anytime they wanted it. In Alaska, and Haines in particular, a lot of material and items they wanted were just not available. The delivery of items from the lower forty-eight states was largely dependant on the Alaskan weather. As they soon found out, Alaskan weather is not dependable. It is, in fact, very unpredictable. They learned a little bit about the "make do" attitude that is so necessary in "The Last Frontier".

There weren't enough rental units around town to house all the cast and crew so people were moving out of their houses and in with friends so they could rent out their houses at an inflated price. A few of the locals made decent money that way.

One of the first mistakes the film company made was not shooting their winter scenes right away when we had a good snow. They waited until our snow melted off and then didn't have the snow they needed. They solved their problem quite cleverly. Instant mashed potato flakes blown about by large fans simulated a realistic blizzard. After the shoot, the potato flakes were left on the ground. You can imagine the mess that soon developed in that wet weather.

I received a phone call one day from a film representative. They wanted to shoot a scene of wolves chasing rabbits. The wolves wouldn't actually be chasing the rabbits, of course. They would be filmed separately and the film would then be spliced together to show a "chase".

They didn't want to use domestic rabbits with pink eyes. They needed to use wild rabbits for authenticity, as they wanted some close-up shots. I had no way of obtaining wild rabbits for them and told them so.

They then put out a notice that they would pay anyone who would like to trap some rabbits and bring them in. Several of the locals jumped on that deal and put out live traps. After two weeks of checking traps, one man caught one rabbit. He brought it in to them. He got so irate when they offered him five dollars for his two-week's work, he opened the cage and turned it loose. Their plan failed.

They called me again to discuss options. They finally decided what their next step would be. Their representative told me, and this is the honest truth, that they had located an outfit in California that would make brown contact lenses, which could be fitted, to domestic rabbits, thereby giving them the necessary brown eyes. I don't know for sure, but I later heard that that is what they ended up doing.

In order to film "White Fang" the crew built a replica gold rush town on the Chilkat River complete with a stern-wheeler and all the appropriate buildings. Some of those buildings were saved and are now located on the state fair grounds at Haines.

The completed movie was well done and is definitely worth seeing. Some of the local residents worked as extras in the movie. Most people agree, however, that the best part of the movie is the spectacular scenery.

*****

During our four years in Haines, we were seldom able to see our son, Chad, who was living in Anchorage and beginning his career in cartooning. We missed him and felt that we wanted to share in this exciting time of his life.

There was an opening in at the Anchorage post. We put in for it and got the transfer. We sold our Haines home and moved to Eagle River, just fifteen minutes out of Anchorage, in May of 1992.

Author with Haines patrol vehicle
(Photo by Bill Moomey)

# ANCHORAGE '92

We were glad to be back in our old stomping grounds around Anchorage and the Matanuska Valley. We enjoyed, in particular, being part of Chad's life again.

Anchorage headquarters is a big outfit with a lot of blue shirt troopers, a lot of brown shirts troopers and, unfortunately, a lot of supervisors. Most of us felt that we would have a more efficient and streamlined organization with more troops and fewer supervisors. The Anchorage brown shirts were a good group of guys to work with and my last two years with the department were spent there working with them.

The fall and winter seasons gave us a chance to work the hunting seasons, moose poaching, people harassing moose and moose harassing people. We also had our share of bear problems. The remainder of the year, starting about June, kept us busy working the popular and varied sport fisheries. We had all five species of the pacific salmon including pink, red, silver, chum and king salmon. We had an incredibly large patrol area requiring the use of four-wheel-drive vehicles, four-wheelers, riverboats and aircraft. We had a sergeant, four Fish and Wildlife Troopers and three Fish and Wildlife Enforcement Officers (FWEO's). The enforcement officers had limited authority, but could enforce the hunting and fishing regulations.

Some of our more active fishery areas were the Susitna River drainages in the Susitna Valley. These included the Yentna River, Alexander Creek, Deshka River and other tributaries. These are all beautiful salmon-rich waterways, which cannot be reached by vehicle. You can get to these fisheries by airplane or by boat. We used both. Occasionally we worked the Skwentna River, which empties into the Yentna River, which in turn empties into the Susitna River, which dumps into the Cook Inlet.

Each one of these creeks and rivers had its own special runs of salmon and an entire book could be written about these creeks and rivers and their fisheries. This author does not pretend to have the expertise nor the inclination to cover the subject in this book.

Our patrols of these rivers were conducted basically by riverboat. Sometimes we flew over and picked up our riverboat that we kept over there. Other times we tried to hit the tide just right and run a riverboat the thirty miles across Cook Inlet from Anchorage to the mouth of Susitna River. From there, we could run upstream to the other creeks.

I would not recommend anyone using a riverboat to cross Cook Inlet. It's a dangerous piece of water and there were several times I questioned our wisdom. We went because we felt obligated to go, but we had some bad experiences out there ranging from nearly being swamped by rough water to getting fogged in and being unable to find our way to the mouth of the Susitna. We always managed to get over there one way or another to get the job done.

*****

On one particular assignment, I was dropped off by floatplane on Alexander Lake. I unloaded my inflatable rubber boat with wooden floorboards and was to float the length of Alexander Creek. I was in plain clothes and would contact fishermen on the way downstream. I would be picked up at the mouth of the creek in two days.

The float trip down turned out to be a marathon. There were no fishermen on the first half of the creek. It was all brushy and heavily treed wilderness. Many trees had toppled over across the creek making it necessary for me to haul the boat and all my camp gear up some steep banks, over past the trees and back down to the water. I had about a half dozen of those portages. It was exhausting work in the hot weather and the endless amount of mosquitoes didn't help make it any more enjoyable.

On my first night on the river, I found a wide gravel bar on a sweeping bend. It was firm, level and dry with plenty of room for a tent and small campfire. I fished for trout for a couple of hours that evening, releasing several, until I finally caught one that was big enough for a hearty supper. If I had realized that I wouldn't have time to fish the next night, I would have kept the small fish for then.

After a supper of fresh fried trout and corn on the cob (cooked in hot coals) I was watching the last burning embers and thinking about the next day's plans. I saw a movement out of the corner of my eye and looked over to see, on the other side of the creek, a black bear walking the riverbank and dividing his attention between looking over at me and following the trail in front of him. He was obviously following something.

The bear turned and went into the woods leaving me to believe I would not see him again. I was wrong. About a hundred yards upstream I heard some brush cracking and saw a cow and calf moose come running out, splash across the creek and continue into the trees. It was only a few moments before "Blackie" came out at the same spot, crossed the creek and was hot on their trail. I listened but never heard anything further. A bear's success at downing a moose calf with the cow present is not always assured.

The next morning, I continued downstream and finally broke into more open country and away from the deadfalls.

I started running into groups of fishermen. I stopped and checked all their licenses and their catch. Sometimes I would pull into the bank before reaching them and fish for a short while so I could observe their fishing techniques and learn where they were putting their fish after catching them.

Alexander Creek gets a lot of alien fishermen who rent cabins down near the creek mouth and rent riverboats to come upstream to the prime fishing spots. Sometimes they will take their day's limit of king salmon back to the lodge freezer and return for another limit. They'll try to go back to their home country with a large number of king salmon where they can sell them easily for two hundred dollars apiece. When I retired from the Department in 1994, we were still trying to perfect a method of preventing those over-limits. It's difficult when you have hundreds of fishermen going back and forth to several lodges, dozens of cabins and numerous tent camps. It's especially difficult when you have only one trooper, or even two or three, working the area.

*****

We had a large white wall tent with two bunks set up for the summer on the Susitna River just a short distance from Alexander Creek. It was somewhat hidden from view, as was our riverboat. It was a comfortable camp and was only a few minutes from the fishery.

Alexander Creek has always had a large population of black bears, as do all the creeks and rivers in that part of the country. We had been having problems with a bear, which was regularly getting into our camp and tent while we were gone. We had been very careful about proper disposal of garbage, etc. I think that cooking in a tent causes the tent

160

canvas to soak up food odors and that is probably what that bear was smelling.

We knew it would only be a matter of time before the bear came in while we were there. The last thing we wanted was to kill a bear and would only do so if our lives were threatened.

The bear came back. One of the enforcements officers and I were asleep on our army cots. The bear's snuffling and grunting woke us up. The bear started scratching at the front tent flap and we both had our handguns ready. There was just enough light in the sky for the enforcement officer to see the outline of the bear through the gap in the tent flap. He fired a .357 round over the bear's head. The bear took off and we went out the front of the tent to hear him crashing through the brush some distance away. Shortly after that, the fishing season was over, we removed our camp and never did have to harm the bear.

*****

Both black and brown bears seem to like the town of Anchorage. Occasionally they had to be killed, but usually we were able to chase them back into a wooded area or tranquilize them with a dart gun and transport them to another area. I said "we", but I need to give credit to the Alaska Department of Fish and Game who normally did the biggest share of that with our assistance. Alaska Fish and Game has some excellent biologists who are dedicated to the protection of all the wild creatures. Their jobs, like ours, are often misunderstood by the public and they often take heat they don't deserve. They don't always receive the recognition and credit they do deserve. After working closely with the Fish and Game biologists for twenty years, I have a lot of respect for them.

\*\*\*\*\*

A call came into the Anchorage office one day reporting a bull moose that had been poached out of season and in an area used by hikers and people hoping to get a glimpse of a wild animal. The license plate number of the suspect was given. One of the enforcement officers received the call and the case was given to him. Bob was an excellent and talented enforcement officer and he did a great job of working the case, as we all knew he would.

One of the other troopers and I hiked up into the area and located the moose. He had a huge sixty-inch rack. We took photos and made a thorough search of the area. He had been killed with an arrow. Bob conducted a very professional investigation and was able to make a good case against the suspect. The suspect then confessed to the poaching. He was a professional firefighter out of Anchorage and an experienced archer. When the news broke, he quickly became one of the most detested men in Anchorage. The public was outraged with him. He had taken his young nephew who was visiting from out of state with him on the poaching. That made the violation even worse. Between being chastised by the archery club, problems with his co-workers at the fire station and the severe sentencing by the court, he paid a heavy price for his indiscretion.

\*\*\*\*\*

Moose are beautiful animals. They are impressive in size and are well designed for what is demanded of them in daily life. They have been called ugly by some people, but I think they are mistaken. I still get excited, even today, when I see a moose. Do not underestimate a moose. They may look tame and docile, but they have been responsible for the deaths of several people in Alaska and the trampling of many others.

A woman was trampled and killed in her Anchorage back yard just before I retired and left the department. A man was killed on the Anchorage college campus just after I retired. There have been many other incidents involving moose. Moose are unpredictable as are most wild animals.

*****

During the spring of 1993 I was assigned to patrol by snow machine our portion of the Iditarod Trail during the Iditarod Dogsled Race. The Iditarod race is 1,049 miles long and it takes the fastest dog teams approximately twelve days to run it from Anchorage to Nome.

One of the enforcement officers went with me and our job was to keep the moose off the dog sled trail, among other things. The goal was to minimize, as much as possible, the musher/moose conflicts, which were becoming prevalent.

Bob and I stopped at the supermarket and loaded up with groceries. We drove north of Anchorage and unloaded our snow machines out of Wasilla. We ran the machines west to the Susitna River and up the River. Dark found us still moving and following the Yentna River. Then it started snowing which decreased visibility and made navigation difficult. If we became careless and made a wrong move, there was a potential for injury. We finally came to a spot on the river, which we knew was directly across from our department cabin. We shot across the snow covered ice and soon had a fire going in the cozy cabin. We slept well that night.

The next morning we headed up to Skwentna and began seeing large numbers of dog teams coming in. Before long there were dozens of teams tied up at the Skwentna stopover. Bob and I made our presence known by patrolling the area and conversing with the mushers. Most of them seemed glad to see us around. There had been several problems there in the past. In addition to various moose problems, spectators on snow machines would show up and run their machines around all night disturbing the mushers and their dogs who were trying to sleep. The large amount of dog food that was dropped off at this rest stop was partially used on the spot and then some was taken on the sleds for the next leg of the trip. The surplus dog food was sold later and the money was donated to a children's organization. In previous years the less desirable snow machiners were actually stealing the dog food and taking it back home for their dogs. We all thought that was stooping pretty low.

Bob and I were quite pleased that, because of our presence, there were none of the usual problems and things went smoothly for the mushers.

*****

Dressing properly for a snow machine patrol in Alaska can be very challenging. At times you'll be colder than a pipeliner's butt and other times you'll be working up a sweat. We learned to dress in layers and to stay cool enough to avoid sweating. Once you get wet, it is difficult to stay warm. My favorite glove system was a pair of lightweight wool military gloves under a pair of leather choppers. The combined pair are plenty warm for riding, but by removing the choppers, the wool gloves allow you to work with gear or equipment.

One of the very real dangers of winter snow machine patrol was getting into overflow. Overflow occurs in very cold weather. In some places on the river the water freezes to the bottom which forces the oncoming water to squeeze up through the holes or cracks and run on top of the ice. This water can then glaze over and appear to be firm ice. If you break through the ice with a snow machine, the rubber track can get wet and freeze making the machine inoperable. If you go through deep enough to get yourself wet, the only thing you can do is get a fire going as quickly as possible and dry out.

Overflow also occurs on lakes when the weight of the snow pushes the ice downward, squeezing the water up on top of the ice. The water lays hidden between the ice and the snow. Many people have suffered frostbite or died due to overflow. It follows then that anytime you operate snow machines, especially on rivers or lakes, you should keep matches and fire starting material handy.

I always recommend to snow machiners in deep snow areas to keep a pair of snowshoes on board. There are some wonderful compact and lightweight snowshoes on the market now. It can be fatal to have your machine quit and leave you stranded in waist-deep snow.

One last tip I should mention to anyone starting out new at snow machining is to always keep in mind that early on cold mornings the snow may be firm and crisp enabling you to cover a long distance in a short period of time. During the day, the sun can change the consistency of the snow into a soft, wet, slushy mess. Your machine may bog down and actually be unable to get you back. Solution: always carry survival gear in case of an unexpected overnight stay until the snow firms up again.

*****

One warm, summery day I was working across the Cook Inlet on the Chuitna River with one of the enforcement officers. It was king salmon season and the Chuitna had plenty of them coming up to spawn.

Casey and I had heard rumors that some of the helicopters that were bringing fishermen into the area were engaged in illegal activities such as dropping them off in closed areas and flying out overlimits of king salmon. While checking the river for fishermen, we heard a helicopter operating on a stretch of the river off in the distance.

We started hiking through the brush toward where we had heard the chopper. Luckily, we were wearing our hip boots as we ended up having to go through a wet, muddy marsh to get there. Casey, being much younger and more energetic than me, went on ahead. I caught up with him on the other side of the marsh.

Being unable to keep up with him made me think about how things had changed over the years. I didn't have the stamina I once had and I apparently wasn't willing to push myself beyond my limits as I used to. Our goal here was to reach that helicopter as soon as possible before it left the area.

It was an important goal and several years ago, in order to accomplish it, I would have kept up my pace. I would have broken out in a hard sweat, my legs would be aching and my heart pounding wildly. Still, I would not have slowed down until we got there. Now I was getting tired quicker and after a little bit of sweating and exertion, it was easier to slow down and catch my breath than to keep up the pace. So that's what I did. It made only a couple of minutes difference in time when I got there and had no effect on the outcome of the situation, but it could have.

It confirmed my suspicions that it was time for me to retire and make room for the younger guys to step in and continue the never-ending battle to protect Alaska's wildlife and fish. But, for now, there was the task at hand.

Casey and I reached the brush at the edge of the gravel bar just fifty feet from the helicopter. We saw three men fishing in the river and one or two of them were illegally trying to snag salmon. The chopper pilot was standing nearby watching them. We approached the fishermen and began a conversation. We checked their licenses and began writing citations for the snagging. While we were busy with this, the helicopter pilot quietly sauntered back to the chopper and started it up. It seemed like an odd thing for him to do right at that moment without saying anything about leaving. So I hurried over there and had him shut it back down. He was reluctant at first, but finally did shut it down.

On a hunch, I had him remove the inspection plates on the helicopter floats and guess what! There were three big king salmon inside the floats. He claimed they belonged to three other fishermen he had brought in, but couldn't remember who they were or where he had left them. I cited him for illegal possession of king salmon. He would have been legal if he had provided the names and whereabouts of the owners.

It was pretty obvious what was going on. The three fishermen we had there had caught those fish, stashed them in the floats and were out to catch more. The limit was one king a day. Since no one would admit that they were theirs and the pilot claimed they were someone else's, there was no choice but to cite the pilot. It cost him his job with the helicopter company.

*****

I was approaching the twentieth anniversary of my working for the Department of Public Safety. It had been enjoyable and I was grateful for the opportunities and experiences that the job had provided for me. I was also noticing signs that it was about time for me to get out and make room for someone else to get started on their career.

It was not as much fun as it used to be sleeping on the ground, eating freeze-dried food and working in the cold, miserable rain.

I also didn't like the changes I was seeing in the department. Our administration was getting hung up on numbers. Number of hours spent on sport fish patrol and commercial fish patrol, number of hours spent on other activities and number of citations written. We were being pressured to write more citations and were losing the freedom we once had of spending time getting to know the locals in different areas.

I think being a good Wildlife Protection Trooper or game warden requires getting to know the people in problem areas. I didn't normally write citations to sportsmen unless I figured they really deserved it. That left my numbers pretty low compared to some of the newer troops who were writing every violation they saw as they were directed to do by their supervisors.

I also didn't like the computers that were taking over our lives. It had become a necessity to do all our reports on the computer. I'm kind of old-fashioned and preferred doing mine longhand. I have done everything I could to avoid computers. I was used to doing my reports in the patrol car out in the field or after I got home from work. Now, when I felt like I should be back out in the field, I was stuck in the office at the computer typing up reports. I didn't join the department to be sitting at a desk in front of a computer and it really did irk me.

I was open minded enough to realize that computers were here to stay and that the new troops would feel right at home with them. Their reports would look more professional than our handwritten ones. I still despised computers and that made it difficult for me to learn. I just plain wanted nothing to do with them.

With all the new changes in the department, my decision was easy to make. I would retire and make way for a younger, more energetic computer whiz.

I retired on September 1, 1994. The office threw a going away picnic for Linda and me at Mirror Lake where we ate, canoed and played volleyball. I would like to thank all those who made it a very memorable day including the Palmer and Anchorage personnel. I would especially like to thank my sergeant, Bruce Lester, who had arranged the picnic for us. I had several exceptional sergeants during my career and he was one of them.

# RETIREMENT

Upon my retirement, we immediately moved to Peck, Idaho, where Linda and I live today. We selected this area because of the short, mild winters and the relatively low cost of living. There is lots of wilderness country here in Idaho that is similar to Alaska. That's an added benefit.

We consider ourselves very lucky to have close Alaskan friends living down here near us. Woody and Colleen Bausch and their family live here in the Orofino area. We have also been able to keep in touch with Dick and Korlyn Williams and other close friends in Alaska.

Oh, there are some things I miss about Alaska; some of the people and places. But right now, we're enjoying it here in Idaho. It's like a paradise for us with the mountains and big timber with the mild climate. There's a great steelhead river just a mile from our house and a beautiful fifty-four mile long lake a few miles away.

We will be going back up to Alaska each summer to spend time with family and friends. Being away from Alaska would be a lot harder for me if it weren't possible to go back up occasionally.

We spent our first twenty-five years of life in Michigan, our second twenty-five years in Alaska and our third twenty-five years will probably be spent here in Idaho. I have no idea where the following twenty-five years will find us, but I'll leave a forwarding address.

At this writing, our oldest son, Darin, lives in Fairbanks and is the father of three daughters. He enjoys the Fairbanks area. Darin is a computer systems technician for a large clinic.

Chad lives in Anchorage with his wife, Jennie. He is a very talented artist and produces the well-known comic strip "Tundra". Chad has had nine books of his cartoons published and has recently done artwork for the Alaska Department of Public Safety and for the U.S. Department of the Navy.

Ty is now twenty-four years old and has graduated from the University of Idaho with a Bachelor of Science degree in journalism and mass communication.

I feel like my life has already been full and complete with more than my share of excitement and adventure. Even if I were to die tomorrow, I'd feel that... Naw, forget it. I'd be really pissed!

I'll always be grateful for the opportunities I've had while working for the Alaska Department of Public Safety. They were plenty, they were great and they were exciting. After all, I slept with the bears!

# ABOUT THE AUTHOR

Born and raised in Gratiot County, Michigan, Dave Carpenter married his high school sweetheart, Linda Thum. He attended Central Michigan University in Mount Pleasant, Michigan. At the age of twenty-six, he moved his family to Alaska where they spent the next twenty-five years. Twenty of those years were spent working for the Department of Public Safety. They were twenty years of excitement, adventure and danger. Dave attended the University of Alaska and received his Police Administration degree from that institution. He retired from the Department of Public Safety in 1994 and is a lifetime member of the Fraternal Order of the Alaska State Troopers.

Dave and Linda now reside in Peck, Idaho, where Dave is a volunteer member of the Clearwater County Sheriff's Posse. Dave and Linda continue their annual trips to Alaska to visit their sons and families and some longtime friends. Their trip to Alaska in the fall of 2002 was their seventeenth time for driving the famous Alaska Highway.

Printed in the United States
1180100004B/342-428